# Treasures of Hidden Racism in Education

# Other Works by Dr. Derrick L. Campbell

**Books**
- *Promoting Positive Racial Teacher Student Classroom Relationships*
- *Promoting Positive Racial Teacher Student Classroom Relationships: Workbook*
- *Promoting Positive Racial Teacher Student Classroom Relationships: Methodology*
- *Leading Your Marriage into the Promised Land*
- *Leading Your Marriage into the Promised Land: Workbook for Husbands*
- *Leading Your Marriage into the Promised Land: Workbook for Wives*
- *Advanced Marriage Training for Singles*
- *Husband Leadership Principles*
- *Advanced Marriage Training for Couples: Workbook*

**Education Articles**
- *Cultural Influences: Differences in Teacher Perspectives*
- *Developing Student Recognition Programs for Historically Underserved Students*
- *Ethical Leadership Develops Moral Communities*
- *Firing the Principal Does Not Guarantee Improvement*
- *Leadership Qualities that Promote Positive Racial Teacher-Student Relationships*
- *Poverty: The Assumed Link to Low Minority Student Achievement*
- *Reducing Cultural Bullying in Schools*
- *Reducing Cultural Challenges Saves Money*
- *Reducing Inappropriate Special Education Referrals for Historically Underserved Students*
- *Save Money by Reducing Student Suspensions*
- *Smile: They Like It*
- *Steering the Organizational Change Process*
- *Student Input is the Key to Effective Classroom Management*
- *Student Perspectives of Classroom Disruptions*
- *Students Need Professional Development Too*
- *Students Who Promote Positive Racial Teacher-Student Classroom Relationships: Part 1*
- *Students Who Promote Positive Racial Teacher-Student Classroom Relationships: Part 2*
- *Teacher Perspectives of Classroom Disruptions*
- *Teacher Qualities that Promote Positive Racial Classroom Relationships*
- *Transforming Afro-American Content into the School Curriculum*
- *Unions Can Benefit Organizational Change*
- *Classroom Management Strategies*

# Treasures of Hidden Racism in Education

Dr. Derrick L. Campbell, Ed.D.

DLC Consultant Group

All rights reserved. No part of this book may be reproduced in any form or by any electronic or mechanical means, including information storage and retrieval systems, without permission in writing from the publisher, except by a reviewer who may quote brief passages in a review.

Published by Derrick L. Campbell

**First edition: May, 2016**

**ISBN: 978-0-9975052-1-4**

Printed in the United States of America

# TABLE OF CONTENTS

Page

ABOUT THE AUTHOR ............................................vi

Chapter

I. INTRODUCTION ......................................1

II. THE PROBLEM AREAS...............................7

    Teacher Discrimination ..............................7
    Black Student and Hispanic Student
    Beliefs and Perceptions..............................13
    School-Student Racial Disparity................19
    Discrimination in the Classroom ...............33
    Teacher-Student Verbal and
    Non-verbal Behavior..................................59
    Teacher-Student Racial Differences ..........115

III. PROPOSED SOLUTIONS.............................121

    Teacher-Student Relationships ...................121

IV. REFERENCES ...............................................133

## ABOUT THE AUTHOR

Dr. Campbell holds a Bachelor of Science degree in Electronics Engineering Technology from Capital Institute of Technology, a second Bachelor of Science degree in Math Education from the University of the District of Columbia, a Masters in Education Administration from Lincoln University, and a doctoral degree in Educational Leadership from Rowan University.

He is also the founder and CEO of DLC Consultant Group. After authoring his first book, Promoting Positive Racial Teacher-Student Classroom Relationships, in January 2008, Dr. Campbell developed a Cultural Relationship Training Program that improves teacher-student classroom relationships as well as several companion programs. He also developed the B.O.S.S. Leadership Training Program that improves manager-employee workplace relationships and relationships between Law Enforcement and their local community.

Dr. Campbell authored his second book, Leading Your Marriage into the Promised Land, in February 2009. Leading Your Marriage into the Promised Land educates the husband on a leadership process that ensures the husband and wife work together as a team. The husband and wife work together to develop and implement agreed upon goals that embrace the different values that they learn as children. Following the writing of this book, he wrote two companion workbooks, one for husbands and the other for wives.

Dr. Campbell authored his fifth book - Advanced Marriage Training for Singles - in September, 2014. Advanced Marriage Training for Singles better equips singles to make informed decisions about who they marry before they decide to become engaged.

In 2016, he authored Advanced Marriage Training for Couples: Workbook and Husband Leadership Principles.

Dr. Campbell is founder and president of The Promised Land Ministry. The Promised Land Ministry provides training for churches, non-profit organizations, men, and couples. Churches and non-profit organizations receive training in the areas of strategic planning, team building, and leadership.

In August 2007, Dr. Campbell founded Leadership Advancement Journal which publishes articles on recent educational, organizational, and business developments that impact our culture. His articles, Reducing Cultural Bullying in Schools and Reducing Inappropriate Special Education Referrals for Historically Underserved Students, have been featured in a local New Jersey newspaper.

In November 2008, Dr. Campbell began the new Radio talk show - Culturally Speaking with Doctor Derrick. On this talk show we discuss the solutions to the cultural challenges that exist in our schools, workplaces, and community. Dr. Campbell has had a host of local and national speakers who contributed to the content of the show.

Dr. Campbell has lectured at various locations throughout the nation, including the National Association for the Advancement of Colored People (NAACP), Iron Sharpens Iron Men's Conference, and local churches. He has ministered to the youth at his home church on the topic of Christian student rights in the public schools and has ministered at another local New Jersey church on Overcoming the Poverty Cycle. He has been a board member of his church's men's ministry, Athletes United in Christ, and has participated in various church activities. He has facilitated Leading Your Marriage into the Promised seminars at churches and the Iron Sharpens Iron Conference Men's Conference.

# Introduction

John follows the same daily routine as he prepares himself for work. However, today is a little different. He begins his day with his coffee and a newspaper. He takes a few sips of his coffee and opens to a newspaper article regarding a recent Gallup poll survey.

To his surprise, the survey results indicate the disparity between the opinions of whites and blacks. The Gallup poll reveals that 59% of all Americans believe that black children have the same educational opportunities as white children do. Furthermore, the same Gallup poll found that 92% of whites feel that educational opportunities for black children have improved since the Brown v. Board of Education decision in 1954, compared with 77% of blacks who feel the same way.

After his children board their bus for school, he begins to reflect on the racial challenges that he had to overcome when he attended school. He thinks to himself: How can I help people to realize that racism in education is real? Even though the Gallup poll surveys serve their purpose, the survey never provides the information regarding why racism in education continues.

He begins his research and finds out that many articles are opinionated. There seems to be a lack of credible research as well as the solution for eliminating racism in education. He becomes disgusted and realizes that the evidence is sparse. Without the evidence, there is no way that anyone may ever know the truth. Herein is the purpose of this book.

The failure to eliminate racism in education rest on the shoulders of many. For more than 62 years, government, state, and private initiatives have failed at eliminating racism in schools. In 1954, the Supreme Court's landmark decision of Brown v. Board of Education banned school segregation and affirmed the right to quality education for all children. The passage of Title VI of the Civil Rights Act of 1964, Title IX of the Education Amendments of 1972, and Section 504 of the Rehabilitation Act of 1973 prohibited discrimination based on race, sex, and disability. In 1965, the Elementary and Secondary Education Act included a set of comprehensive programs which included the Title I program of Federal aid to disadvantaged children to address the problems of poor urban and rural areas. In the same year, the Higher Education Act authorized assistance for postsecondary education that included financial aid programs for needy college students.

Since it is evident that government and state initiatives need enhancements with eliminating racism in education, independent individuals have provided alternatives. For example, former NBA star and sports analyst Magic Johnson has opened several alternative high schools for students, which specialize in helping students who have dropped out or are at-risk of dropping out of school. In 2011, former tennis champion Andre Agassi, founded the Las Vegas-based Andre Agassi College Preparatory Academy Charter School. In 2011, Jalen Rose, who is a former NBA player and current sports broadcaster founded a Detroit-based charter school called the Jalen Rose Leadership Academy (JRLA). In 2012, former NFL star Deion Sanders founded Prime Prep Academy charter school in Texas. In 2013, "Timber," rapper Pitbull opened a Sports and Leadership and Management Academy (SLAM) Charter School in Miami. Racism in education continues to dominate even with the help of United States government and philanthropic individuals.

Racism in education continues to persist as evidenced by the disparities in academic achievement and disciplinary consequences for historically underserved students. According to the National Center for Educational Statistics, white students continue to outperform black students since 1972.

Furthermore, the United States Department of Education Office for Civil Rights reported the disparity between whites and blacks when considering school discipline. This gap begins in preschool. Even though Black children represent 18% of the preschool population, they represent 48% of the out of school suspensions. Comparatively, White students represent 43% of the preschool population, while only representing 26% of the out of school suspensions.

This imbalance of discipline continues through high school. Black students are three times more likely to be suspended from school when compared to White students. The average suspension rate for White students is 5% while the average suspension rate for Black students is 16%.

Additionally, Black girls are suspended at a rate 12% higher when compared to other girls of different ethnicities.

The book - Treasures of Hidden Racism in Education - contains the seminal works of the research that validate the past and present existence of racism in schools. It includes the collection of undeniable research that has been forged to the background. It covers the primary factors that contribute to racism in education that in many cases are either overlooked or dismissed.

The reader will benefit from knowing the actual facts that continue to contribute to racism in education. With this type of knowledge, a true discussion of the solution can begin. Without it, racism in education will continue to run rampant.

## *Teacher Discrimination*

Teachers discriminate against students by stereotyping according to ethnicity. According to Rubovits and Maehr (1973), White females enrolled in a child development course for perspective elementary teachers who taught a lesson to a group of seventh and eighth grade students (a) gave less attention to Blacks, (b) ignored most of the statements made by Black students, (c) praised Black students less, and (d) criticized Black students more. "Research has revealed that teachers form negative, inaccurate, and inflexible expectations based on such attributes as the race and perceived social class of their pupils" (Joint Center for Economic and Policy Studies, Committee on Policy and Racial Justice, 1989, p. 17). White teachers may have difficulty in understanding minorities due to the teachers' rejection of the students' lifestyles (Ornstein & Levine, 1990). Schools have a bias against students who do not share the same characteristics as White, female, middle-class teachers (Washington, 1982).

Teachers are more likely to have negative academic and behavioral expectations regarding Black students compared to expectations of White students (Baron, Tom, & Cooper, 1985). White teachers have more negative attitudes toward Black children (Datta et al., 1968; Leacock, 1969) and rate Black students more negatively (Coates, 1972; Eaves, 1975) compared to White students. White teachers rate Black male children more deviant compared to White children (Eaves, 1975). White teachers direct more criticism toward Black males (Simpsom & Erickson, 1983) and rate Black male children personalities more negatively (Coates, 1972) compared to White male children. White teachers perceive White students more positively compared to Black students (Washington, 1982). High prejudiced White teachers are less pleased with Black students compared to low prejudiced White teachers (Feldman, 1985). White teachers showed a heightened hostility toward brighter Black children (Leacock, 1969). White teachers interact with White gifted and nongifted students more than with gifted and nongifted Black students (Rubovits & Maehr, 1973). In a middle-class White school, White teachers perceived that White student inattention revealed that teachers need to arouse student interest (Leacock, 1969). However, White teachers perceived that the same behavior in Black students resulted from boredom due to limited attention span.

European American teachers favor other students rather than Black students. European Americans have favorable attitudes toward Mexican Americans compared to Blacks and are more likely to accept Mexican Americans compared to Blacks due to Mexican Americans having a closer skin color to European Americans (Burmal, 1970). According to Grossman (1998), "[Black] students who are seen as fun-loving, happy, cooperative, energetic, and ambitious by Black teachers are viewed as talkative, lazy, fun-loving, high-strung, and frivolous by their European-American teachers" (p. 18).

Research reports Black and White teachers have perceptions of students based on their race. Black and White teachers perceive White girls more positively White boys, Black boys, and Black girls (Washington, 1982). Compared to White teachers, Black teachers perceive Black girls more negatively. White teachers perceive Black boys more negatively when compared to Black teachers.

Teachers have perceptions of and reactions to Hispanic students. Traditional classroom teachers may view Hispanic student placement in their classroom as a punishment for them and do not appreciate these children (Ortiz, 1988). Teachers perceive straightforward-acting Hispanic children as arrogant and smart. Ortiz (1988) reports teachers react to Hispanic children after initial introductions by (a) accepting them and training them as others, (b) believing they have dull children who will embarrass them as they cope with them throughout the entire year, or (c) believe these children are better than other children.

## *Black and Hispanic Student Beliefs and Perceptions*

When incorporating students into a marginalized society by slavery, conquest, and colonization, students believe school is detrimental to their identity (Ogbu, 1987, 1992). Indians, Mexican Americans, Puerto Ricans, and Blacks share "the experience of having been brought into the United States society against their will and then relegated to subordinate status" (Ogbu, 1978, p. 255). Blacks, Mexicans, and Puerto Ricans are caste-like immigrants who were involuntarily incorporated into the United States (Ogbu, 1983). Involuntary minorities such as Blacks are not willing to perform well in school due to difficulty with crossing cultural lines (Ogbu, 1992). "A major reason previous attempts at educational reform have been unsuccessful is that the relationships between teachers and students and between schools and communities have remained essentially unchanged" (Cummins, 1986, p. 18). According to Ogbu (1983), "Blacks have learned since slavery that the way to get ahead even within the limited universe open to them, the status mobility system is not through merit and talent but through white patronage" (p. 177). Americans of color adapt to a society that does not value their ethnicity, history, heritage, or language by establishing societal survival strategies (Shade, 1997). Black parents prepare their children to live in a dual cultural world that involves helping them to develop skills for adult roles such as wage earners and parenthood in addition to negotiating a dominant society that has different cultural values and judges people by their skin color or ethnic background (Zayas & Solari, 1994). Blacks who live in an urban society and a society that dislikes them for the color of their skin ensure they do not become victims by approaching people with caution, wariness, and a sense of distrust (Shade, 1982).

Student perceptions and feelings regarding teachers and themselves influence student achievement. Students do better in school when they believe getting a good education will increase their chances for success (Stienberg, Dornbusch, & Brown, 1992). Students who perceive that teachers have favorable feelings toward them have higher achievement levels when teachers have positive views toward them (Davidson & Lang, 1960). Children who have positive feelings regarding teachers have higher achievement levels. Black and Latino urban high school students believe their underachievement results when they perceive racism and discrimination toward them (Lee, 1999) and become limited by American society (Stienberg et al., 1992). High school Latino students believe school is confusing and punishing, which results in their failure at school (Quiroz, 2001). A little more than half of surveyed Hispanics and non-Hispanic participants agree some Hispanic students have little desire to meet school achievement standards (Grossman, 1995). Black adolescents believe school is a hostile place and teachers are oppression agents (Boykin, 1986). White teachers symbolize the racism Black students have endured throughout their entire lives (Gay & Abrahams, 1972).

Black and Hispanic students have developed teacher beliefs that can affect teacher-student relationship development. Black first graders believe interactive teacher-student relationships are the most important factor in school (Slaughter-Defoe & Carlson, 1996). Black sixth graders believe teachers who think well of them are characterized as democratic, responsive, understanding, kind, adaptable, fair, and optimistic (St. John, 1971). Compared to Hispanic students, Black students perceive that their teachers are more enthusiastic, give more appropriate feedback, pace the class more appropriately, and are more task-oriented (Waxman, 1989). Latino students believe teachers are racist because teachers consistently underestimate the students' competence and intelligence (Patthey-Chavez, 1993). Social scientists agree: "Children learn social, racial, and religious prejudices in the course of observing and being influenced by the existing patterns in the culture which they live" (Clark, 1955, p. 17). Culture conflict for Mexican American children results from requiring language and informational processing style abandonment (Shade, 1997). Exhorting Hispanics to relinquish their values, language, and lifestyles and accept lifestyles that are foreign to them are acceptable practices according to American society. Most Hispanics and non-Hispanic participants surveyed agree educators can motivate Hispanic children to seek their teachers' approval and model themselves to be like them by developing close personal relationships with them (Grossman, 1995).

## *School-Student Racial Disparity*

The cultural mismatch between students and school is the reason for student academic failure (Erickson, 1987, 1997). The attempt at minority student Americanization that involves fixing culturally flawed children by changing their values and language has failed at increasing minority student achievement (Garcia, 2000). The main reason for low minority student achievement in the United States is racism creates a poverty cycle that minority students are unable to break (Ogbu, 1974, 1978, 1982, 1987). Student academic achievement decreases when the difference between the student's culture and the school culture increases and the classroom environment does not value the student's home culture (Heath, 1983). When an educational cultural match is not possible, there must be at least respect and value of the culture that children bring with them (Bourdieu & Passeron, 1979).

Researchers report minority student academic failure resulted from the minorities' economic and societal positions. Subjecting Blacks, Mexican Americans from the southwest region, and Native Americans to American assimilation by slavery, conquest, or colonization results in them taking an oppositional stance to institutions controlled by Whites, which has led to lower achievement and increased dropout rates (Delgado-Gaitan, 1988). Indians, Mexican Americans, Puerto Ricans, and Blacks have received an education that ineffectively prepared them for social and technoeconomic positions in adult life and have faced the job ceiling challenge that reinforces their inferior education and lower school performance (Ogbu, 1978).

When incorporating students into a marginalized society by slavery, conquest, and colonization, students believe school is detrimental to their identity (Ogbu, 1987, 1992). Indians, Mexican Americans, Puerto Ricans, and Blacks share "the experience of having been brought into the United States society against their will and then relegated to subordinate status" (Ogbu, 1978, p. 255). Blacks, Mexicans, and Puerto Ricans are caste-like immigrants who were involuntarily incorporated into the United States (Ogbu, 1983). Involuntary minorities such as Blacks are not willing to perform well in school due to difficulty with crossing cultural lines (Ogbu, 1992). "A major reason previous attempts at educational reform have been unsuccessful is that the relationships between teachers and students and between schools and communities have remained essentially unchanged" (Cummins, 1986, p. 18). According to Ogbu (1983), "Blacks have learned since slavery that the way to get ahead even within the limited universe open to them, the status mobility system is not through merit and talent but through white patronage" (p. 177). Americans of color adapt to a society that does not value their ethnicity, history, heritage, or language by establishing societal survival strategies (Shade, 1997). Black parents prepare their children to live in a dual cultural world that involves helping them to develop skills for adult roles such as wage earners and parenthood in addition to negotiating a dominant society that has different cultural values and judges people by their skin color or ethnic background (Zayas & Solari, 1994). Blacks who live in an urban society and a society that dislikes them for the color of their skin ensure they do not become victims by approaching people with caution, wariness, and a sense of distrust (Shade, 1982).

Distrust between schools and Blacks results from hostile treatment of Blacks and discrimination in schools (Ogbu, 1983). According to Farkas, Grobe, and Shaun

(1990), employment discrimination is the primary source of Black student opposition to schooling. "Interviews with students reveal that culturally diverse students feel that they are not being educated to live in a racially and culturally diverse society" (Leiding, 2006, p. 263). Blacks believe schools ineffectively prepare Black children with the same skills that enable White middle-class persons to attain good jobs and wages (Ogbu, 1978). Blacks discourage school success as a cultural goal and respond by developing survival strategies that contribute to school failure as well as conflict with the schools (Ogbu, 1983). Many culturally diverse children learn how to underachieve due to their keen insight, an ability to note inconsistencies, and sensitivity to social injustices, therefore growing wary and critical of the elitist ideology promoted in schools (Leiding, 2006).

Blacks learn at an early age to be wary of people and systems in their environment (Shade, 1978; Wubberhorst, Graford, & Willis, 1971). Social scientists agree: "Children learn social, racial, and religious prejudices in the course of observing, and being influenced by, the existence of patterns in the culture in which they live" (Clark, 1955, p. 17). Black students who develop oppositional social identities that involve developing distrust for Whites and dislikes for behaviors associated with being White may resist academic achievement because it is associated with White culture (Fordham & Ogbu, 1986; Ogbu, 1988). Gilbert and Gay (1985) reported that "the collision of the school culture with the Black culture on the procedures that surround teaching and learning can have devastating effects on both teachers' and students' academic efforts and achievements" (p. 136). Black youth perceive the opportunity structure differently from Whites and consequently put less effort and commitment into their schoolwork (Ogbu, 1978). Schools can work effectively with culturally diverse students by having (a) an ethnic and multicultural curriculum, (b) teacher training in a multicultural curriculum, (c) strong instructional leadership, (d) high expectations for all students, (e) a safe, orderly, warm, concerning, appreciative student learning environment, (f) emphasis on basic skills, (g) continuously monitoring of student progress, (h) clear and balanced goals, (i) high teacher and student morals, and (j) respect for individual differences (Leiding, 2006). Minorities groups tend to be in a dominated relationship with the majority group when victimized by widespread school failure (Ogbu, 1978).

Schools encompass cultural expectations that present challenges for Black students. Schools and Black student conflict result from expectation differences (Gilbert

& Gay, 1985). "The lack of cultural synchronization and negative teacher expectations result in hidden and often unintended conflict between teachers and their students" (Irvine, 1990, p. xviii). Black sixth-grade students believe fluent, confident, broad, and stimulating teachers do not think well of them (St. John, 1971). Black students believe White teachers have low estimates of the students' ability and worth (Davidson & Lang, 1960). Black students believe their teachers are more prejudiced toward them when compared to White students and indicate a strong feeling of rejection (Amos, 1952). White teachers rate Black students more negatively when compared to White students (Coates, 1972; Eaves, 1975). Students want teachers to recognize them in such a way that they feel important (Norton, 1995). Minority students reach higher achievement levels when they feel positive toward the dominant culture as well as their own (Bourdieu &

Passeron, 1979; Cummins, 1986). Teachers who are culturally different from their students have a greater challenge creating a trusting environment when cultural diversity and race factors are not put on the table by the school and students perceive these factors as important to their identity and school success (Weiner, 2003). According to Gilbert and Gay (1985), "school leaders must stop operating on the assumption that all the reasons for Black children's problems with school rest with the children and accept the fact that much of the responsibility rests with the school system" (p. 136). Black student academic performance increases when they perceive that teachers and other school personnel are supportive and helpful (Patchen, 1982; Pollard, 1989).

Many school social codes are unfamiliar and opposed to culturally diverse student home codes (Leiding, 2006). Blacks have difficulty with school instructional concepts and ideas that are absent in their community, culture, or economic environment that ignore or misrepresent their present condition (Gordon, Miller, & Rollock, 1990). School instructional procedures include cultural values, orientations, and perceptions that differ from those of Black students (Gilbert & Gay, 1985). Inappropriate curriculum and instruction are concerns that make reversing underachievement for culturally diverse students difficult (Leiding, 2006). "Most elementary and secondary school curricula are oriented towards white middle-class children" (Sedlacek & Brooks Jr., 1976, p. 48). Public schools continue to have culturally based philosophies and curricula that focus on White European and Judeo-Christian values (Valverde, 2006). Improving school for Black students includes establishing a functional partnership between Black culture and school culture and developing school educational missions that do not compromise or ignore the cultural identity of Black children (Gilbert & Gay, 1985). Effective high school instructional programs place value on the students' language and culture (Lucas, Henze, & Donato, 1990). Instructional materials and instructors who work well for European students do not necessarily work well for culturally diverse students, and to believe that they do is to assume Black, Latino, American Indian, Asian, Arab and African immigrants, and European-origin students have identical personal, social, cultural, historical, and family traits (Leiding, 2006).

School instructional procedures include cultural values, perceptions, and orientations that differ from those of Black students (Gilbert & Gay, 1985). Students who are not interested in school may meet teacher demands for compliance with resistance (Bidwell, 1965). Blacks acquire cultural values, attitudes, and learning styles that conflict with values, attitudes, and learning styles needed for success in public schools (Ogbu, 1978). Exposing minority students to conditions such as limited parental access to economic and educational resources, conflicting ideas about cultural transmission and primary language use in the home, and interaction style that does not prepare students for typical teacher-student interaction patterns prepare students for school failure before they begin to attend school. Individuals who accept school cultural orientation values expect passivity by the learner, authoritative transmission of information by the teacher, individual effort aimed at completing assigned tasks, performance recognition, avoidance of confrontations, and minimal antagonisms (Dreeben, 1968). In school, students become passive informational recipients while in their culture they are involved in a learning experience that is give and take, and in one situation, they may be the learner and in another situation, they are the teacher (Gay & Abrahams, 1972). Black students can benefit from teachers who show concern and care for students by establishing family- and community-like classroom environments that include telling personal anecdotes, using relevant course material, and modifying interaction styles that entertain and engage students (Howard, 2001).

## *Discrimination in the Classroom*

Discrimination against marginalized students is a persistent problem in classrooms throughout the United States (Garcia, 1984). "Race has long been acknowledged as having a major effect upon the teaching process and classroom situation" (Feldman, 1976, p. 20). Classroom interaction studies have found teachers discriminate against students who are not White, male, and middle class (Entwise & Webster, 1974; Safilios-Rothchild, 1979). White teachers create classroom problems when they interpret culture as a limitation to student progress (Powell & Caseau, 2004).

A cultural mismatch between the traditional classroom structure and Latino cultural norms exists (Garcia & Guerra, 2003). Most surveyed Hispanics and non-Hispanic participants agree Hispanic students are accustomed to cultural foods, music, holidays, language, and customs that may become cause for Hispanic difficulty in relating to Anglo-oriented classrooms (Grossman, 1995). Mexican American parents allow children to decide how to carry out a task and when it should be completed, while in school, teachers control how, when, and what materials are used to complete the task (Delgado-Gaitan, 1987). Voluntary minorities such as Hispanics are willing to conform to classroom rules to attempt to overcome difficulties in school because crossing cultural lines is an advantage to survival (Ogbu, 1992). Latino (Delgado-Gaitan, 1992, 1994; Suarez-Orozco, 1989; Tapia, 1998) and Puerto Rican (Hidalgo, 1994; Rubio, 1995; Tapia, 1998) families value education, and Mexican American parents highly value the United States educational system because they believe that it will provide economic mobility for their children (Delgado-Gaitan, 1992). Student school performance correlates with ethnic differences in cultural values placed on educational success (Sue & Okazi, 1990). Diffusing the cultural mismatch between Latino American students and schools results form Latino American parents' awareness that America can assist their children in surviving.

When cultural awareness between White teachers and Black students is absent, the impending result is interference with effective instructional processes caused by frustration and alienation between White teachers and Black students (Gay, 1975). Black students have difficulty accepting teachers as the primary source of knowledge due to becoming accustomed to sharing information on an equal basis with adults rather than the adult teaching them (Gay & Abrahams, 1972). Teachers treat Black high school students as though they are incapable decision makers that require their permission to do everything even though the student has had experience caring for younger brothers and sisters, teaching them safety and personal hygiene skills, and taking care of the home (Gay & Abrahams, 1972). Black students withdraw from the instructional process or become discontented with whatever the teacher does when the teacher hinders student spontaneity and enthusiasm and punishes the student by requiring the student to raise his or her hand in order to be recognized. According to Gay and Abrahams (1972), Black students "react to the teacher not so much as a person but as a member of a group which is defined primarily by skin tone and other physical attributes – just as they are used to being reacted to" (p. 81). Many teachers do not expect Black students to (a) have a short attention span, (b) be easily distracted, (c) fail to complete tasks, (d) speak without raising their hands, (e) wait to be called on, (f) be impulsive in their responses rather than reflective, (g) need a great amount of physical contact, (h) interrupt class by talking to their neighbors, and (i) to experience difficulty with learning materials (Shade, 1994).

Teaching Black students requires creating a culturally compatible classroom that concentrates on developing motivation rather than classroom discipline and management techniques and the teaching process of handling material as well as content (Shade, 1997). Teachers can reach all of their students when they understand the ways in which culture influences the educational process (Powell & Caseau, 2004). How students perceive and react to their classroom instructions may be more important in terms of influencing student outcomes than the quality of teaching behavior (Knight & Waxman, 1991; Walberg, 1976; Winne & Marx, 1977, 1982). Black students will continue to carry their own culture into the classroom, and they will continue to misunderstand their middle-class teacher as profoundly as she or he misunderstands them (Gay & Abrahams, 1972).

Students who find their culture and learning styles reflected in instruction are more likely to be motivated and less likely to be disruptive (Kuykendall, 1992). In order for culturally different students to succeed in the classroom or school, students are required to assimilate by giving up their learning style preference that results from the teacher not modifying their instruction (Leiding, 2006). Schools and Black student conflict develop from expectation differences related to student learning styles (Gilbert & Gay, 1985). Teachers who perceive that students have the same cognitive learning style—field dependent or field independent—are more likely to give better grades to those students (DiStefano, 1970). Good teachers adjust their teaching to serve populations that are culturally and linguistically diverse, which includes incorporating culturally responsive pedagogy by adjusting teaching strategies according to individual learning styles (Villegas, 1991). According to Leiding (2006), "teachers who are sensitive to various cultures will learn about students' backgrounds and ensure that they are aware of relevant information about cultural traditions, religious practices, and patterns of interaction that may affect a students' classroom participation" (p. 279). When teachers realize that learning takes place across cultural media, then teachers adapt teaching to fit student needs (Marchesani & Adams, 1992; Villegas, 1991).

When teachers refuse to customize their instruction to fit student cultural and learning style needs the result can develop a classroom environment that is diametrically opposed to the students.

The highly regimented and formalized school setting is diametrically opposed to Black students' learning experiences (Gay & Abrahams, 1972). Black children believe people in the school are more important than the school concept (Damico, 1983) and place a higher emphasis on people, particularly teachers, rather than school physical aspects (Shade, 1994). Blacks learn at an early age to be wary of people and systems within their environment (Halpern, 1973; Shade, 1978; Wubberhorst et al., 1971) and become socialized to concentrate on people or the social learning aspects (Young, 1974). Blacks believe they should interact with other non-Black Americans by being "careful and watch what people tell you, be careful and watch what you say, and whites are not always on your side" (Orbe, 1994, p. 291). Black students determine their involvement in the learning environment by relying on their perception of the teacher and the affective aspects of the environment (Shade, 1994). Black children are more likely to concentrate on the people involved in the teaching and learning process rather than completing the tasks' requirements (Shade, 1983). Schools require Black students to demonstrate achievement by writing, which requires Black students to transition from demonstrating by oral or dramatic expression activities that Black students are more comfortable with and more likely to have higher achievement levels (Gilbert & Gay, 1985). Verbal learning and written demonstration are consistent with mainstream American and European student mastery that is contrary to culturally different student learning styles (Leiding, 2006). Blacks prefer affective materials (Rychlak, 1975), warm and supportive teachers (St. John, 1971), and a socially interactive environment (Cureton, 1978; Slavin, 1983).

Researchers report Blacks have learning preferences that can influence teacher-student classroom relationships.

Blacks do well on tasks that require auditory sensory involvement but have challenges when the tasks require visual perception (Hall & Kaye, 1977). Blacks categorize pictorial representations in a more relational or holistic manner rather than an analytical or detailed manner (Sigel, Anderson, & Shapiro, 1966). Black students are more likely to learn and recall words that represent concepts that they like compared to words that represent concepts that they dislike (Rychlak, 1975; Rychlak, Hewitt, & Hewitt, 1973). Blacks prefer (a) tactile hands-on learning activities (Shade, 1989), (b) affective materials to facilitate their learning (Rychlak, 1975), (c) approximate time, number, and space activities (Locke, 1992), and (d) sort word lists by their functional value (Orasanu, Lee, & Scribner, 1979). Work that is relevant to present time or future time motivates Blacks (Jenkins & Bainer, 1990) while they prefer to focus on present time rather than future time

(Patton, Warring, Frank, & Hunter, 1993), and value people focus over time focus. The degree of relevance and applicability of the material seem to influence Black learning and are influenced by a preference for deductive rather than inductive reasoning (Shade, 1997). Blacks are not good problem solvers (Jensen, 1969). When teachers require only cognitive activities, Black students feel the request is unnatural and have difficulty following the teacher's request, which results in frustration and withdrawal for Black students (Gilbert & Gay, 1985). When Black students do not honor the teacher's request to participate in cognitive activities, teachers perceive that Black students lack preparation or ability. Black have different and similar learning preferences when compared to Hispanic.

Researchers report Hispanics has learning preferences that can influence teacher-student classroom relationships. According to Leiding (2006), instructional strategies that work with Hispanic and Latino students include (a) using an overhead projector and video clips to help students visualize the instructional material, (b) letting students sit where they please as long as they do not become behavioral problems, (c) giving constant praise, (d) explaining directions in many ways, (e) giving demonstrations, (f) having patience to repeat directions, (g) using hands-on materials, and (h) extending time for assignments and tests. Most surveyed Hispanics and non-Hispanic participants agree educators should provide Hispanic students with short-term assignments (Grossman, 1995). Hispanic students learn by touching, seeing, manipulating, and experiencing concrete objects rather than discussing or reading about ideas. Hispanic students desire to work at a relaxed pace even if it means completing the task will take longer, and educators should organize

Hispanic students to plan their time so they can complete long-term assignments. Dividing learning activities into segments by days may hinder or be less meaningful to Puerto Rican students (Milburn, 2000). Most surveyed Hispanics and non-Hispanic participants disagree that educators should de-emphasize the use of trial-and-error learning, the inquiry method, and other independent study forms and students' efforts to produce quality work is less important than accomplishing a task (Grossman, 1995). Hispanic and Latino learning styles involve (a) an inclusion approach, (b) cooperative learning, (c) peer tutoring, (d) performance-based learning, and (e) family involvement (Leiding, 2006). Teachers expect Hispanic students to have difficulty with content and respond by having simpler materials for them to master such as drill worksheets rather than using textbook materials (Ortiz, 1988). Teachers often assign Hispanic students worksheets for drill rather than regular class work.

Differences in teacher and student thinking styles can complicate teacher-student relationships. Most teachers in educational institutions have a cognitive style that is not consistent with most Mexican Americans and Blacks (Ramerez & Price-Williams, 1974). Blacks have developed a specific method of organizing and processing information (Shade, 1981) that provides a disadvantage to Blacks in school settings (Cohen, 1969). Black thinking style differs from other groups due to Blacks using the right hemisphere of the brain (TenHouton, 1971). Blacks lack sufficient metacognition strategies or comprehension monitoring skills (Borkowski & Krause, 1983). Black thinking is more holistic, intuitive, and integrative when processing information (Hale, 1982; Hillard, 1989), and Black students approach thinking from an intuitive perspective rather than the logical-mathematical approach (Shade, 1994). Blacks are more analytical regarding concepts and ideas when they evaluate information from their particular orientation (Simmons, 1979). Blacks are highly creative thinkers (Torrance, 1982) who prefer deductive reasoning (Locke, 1992) but have the same reasoning styles as other groups (Smith & Drumming, 1989). Most teachers use a bottom-up sorting approach while Blacks use a top-down approach (Shade, 1997). Culturally diverse students are concrete thinkers while most Whites are abstract and deductive thinkers (Leiding, 2006). Teachers' cognitive teaching styles influence student achievement (Saracho & Dayton, 1980).

Over a period of time, teacher expectations influence student achievement and the social organization of the classroom (Brophy, 1983; Brophy & Good, 1970). Teacher expectations that result in different teacher interaction patterns may affect student achievement (Braum, 1976; Brophy, 1983; Brophy & Good, 1970; Clifton, 1981; Cooper, 1979; Dusek, 1975). The teacher accepts differential expectations, and students complement or reinforce these expectations (Brophy, 1983; Brophy & Good, 1970). When teachers have high expectations for students, students raise their hands more often to answer questions and initiate procedural and work-related interactions (Brophy & Good, 1970). Teachers perceive students whom they enjoy teaching as high achievers who conform, respond warmly, and are not hostile toward them (Brophy & Good, 1974; Good & Brophy, 1972; Willis & Brophy, 1974). Teachers do not have high expectations for students whom they perceive as defiant and disobedient (Willis & Brophy, 1974). Teachers (a) provide low-expectation students with less wait time to respond to questions, (b) call on these students less often, (c) pay less attention to them unless there is a disciplinary challenge with the students, and (d) place their seats farthest away from the teacher (Brophy & Good, 1974). Students have higher achievement when teachers have higher expectations (Rosenthal & Jacobson, 1968).

Cooperative learning structures provide a cultural match for Hispanic students (Moll, 1988). Hispanics value people and relationships over task accomplishment (Morales-Jones, 1998). Most surveyed Hispanics and non-Hispanic participants agree (a) curriculum activities should include community-oriented projects, (b) Hispanic students prefer to work in groups, (c) educators should allow Hispanic students to work together on homework, (d) educators should give equal instructional time to group work as well emphasize group work, and (e) educators should encourage Hispanic students to ask each other for help and arrange for peer tutoring (Grossman, 1995). Most surveyed Hispanics and non-Hispanic participants agree Hispanic students are more cooperative and group oriented when compared to Anglo students, and therefore Hispanic students may allow other students to copy their class work or test in order to show helpfulness, brotherhood, and generosity. Mexican American children attempt to learn collectively and maximize their intellectual exchange and knowledge acquisition by working together on assignments that may result in Mexican American students copying answers from each other (Shade, 1997). Successful high school Hispanic students engage in copying one another's homework (Cordeiro & Carspecken, 1993). Hispanic students believe achievement should be cooperative (Brown, 1999). Teachers often complain Mexican American students copy each other's answers to assignments (Shade, 1997).

Teachers need to realize that constructed classroom collaboration may be more culturally relevant and meaningful to some students (Milburn, 2000). "African American learning seems to be influenced by the social situation in which learning occurs" (Shade, 1997, p. 23). Blacks prefer to work in groups (Shade, Kelly, & Oberg, 1997) and socially interactive environments (Cureton, 1978; Slavin, 1983). Black students do well when the teacher incorporates a socialization learning model (Morgan, 1981) and "will work together to benefit the group" (Gilbert & Gay, 1985, p. 134). Black peer-based cooperation in learning translates into cheating for teachers (Gay & Abrahams, 1972). Teachers may interpret Blacks' natural instinct to seek peer assistance as cheating, copying, or frivolous socializing (Bennett, 1997). Black students work and function better in cooperative, informal, and loosely structured environments where teachers and students work together to achieve a common goal (Gilbert & Gay, 1985). Black students perceive teacher-designed orderly classroom environments as dull, stagnant, and uninteresting. "African American learning seems to be influenced by the preference for active involvement rather than passive receptivity" (Shade, 1997). Black children prefer and need a large variety of information at a constantly changing pace and have little tolerance for monotonous or low-level passive activities (Boykin, 1986). Teachers perceive that Black participation in emotion and movement during classroom activities is unnecessary and may eliminate these instructional opportunities to ensure an orderly classroom environment (Gilbert & Gay, 1985). Teachers may ensure an orderly classroom environment by developing disciplinary strategies.

Teachers discriminate against students by implementing differential discipline (US Commission on

Civil Rights, 1973). Teachers with high percentages of Black students in their classroom are more likely to use an authoritarian classroom management approach (Grossman, 1998). Teachers react to Black student learning experiences that are in opposition to traditional public schools by determining Blacks are incapable of following simple rules and therefore make rules that they deem intolerable (Gay & Abrahams, 1972). "They justify this procedure with the belief that these students want to be disciplined and have some order in their lives for a change" (Gay & Abrahams, 1972, p. 77). "Anglo-Americans believed that it was necessary to assure obedience to, in ascending order, their mother, father, government, church, and God" (Spring, 2001, p. 8). Teachers spend more time looking for possible misbehavior by Black students, especially males, and are more prone to respond to Black student behavior by using severe punishments that include corporal punishment and suspensions (Grossman, 1998). The differences between the teachers' backgrounds that teach them to conform to preset externally fabricated rules and regulations and Black street culture tendencies to derive order as a situation happens cause teachers to resort to punishment for petty rules in order to force obedience at the expense of hindering learning (Gay & Abrahams, 1972). Blacks believe middle-class teachers are vulnerable and ignorant regarding Black life, which leaves the teachers at a disadvantage because Black students choose the battlefield, strategy, and weapons, which are words, and they possess a skill that enables them to remain cool in these confrontational situations. Black students believe teachers who telephone parents at home to solve disciplinary challenges have an inability to solve their own problems, and these students lose respect for the teacher. Teacher disciplinary strategies that result in telephoning a parent are ineffective due to Black children learning at a young age to handle their own problems and having the ability to handle their own problems.

Students frequently test the limitations in an inconsistent classroom by ignoring a teacher's first, second, and even third request for compliance; when the teacher decides to deliver a consequence, the student claims the teacher is unfair because the same misbehavior does not always receive the same consequence (Vitto, 2003). "White teachers are right that their Black students are hostile, resent the authority they represent, quick to anger, and have chips on their shoulders" (Gay & Abrahams, 1972, p. 81). Black students react to arbitrary and autocratic White teacher disciplinary assertiveness by believing that a White man is still trying to tell him what to do (Gay & Abrahams, 1972). Most teachers respond to students who attempt to act tough with them by threatening or talking back to the student opposition may result in noncompliant classroom behavior.

Hispanic noncompliant behavior results from instructional challenges, teacher behavior, and gender differences. Most surveyed Hispanics and half of the non-Hispanic participants agree Hispanic students may become anxious, nervous, and rebellious when required to stop working before they have finished their assignment to begin the next tasks with their peers (Grossman, 1998). When successful Hispanic students become resistant, they use class time to do homework for other classes or openly challenge the teacher's authority when teachers display incompetence, prejudice, or an uncaring attitude toward them (Cordeiro & Carspecken, 1993). Most surveyed Hispanics and non-Hispanic participants agree that some Hispanic males may have difficulty complying with female figures due to the patriarchal Hispanic cultural trends student (Spector, 1955). Removing hostile Black students from the classroom only delays the inevitable confrontation between the teacher and the student. Whites attempt to minimize confrontations and struggles with Blacks in the persuasive process that they interpret as divisive while Blacks believe these struggles unify because they care enough to struggle for something (Kochman, 1981). American societal beliefs that posit Blacks as inferior to European-descent Americans result in Blacks' preoccupation and group focus on the concepts of freedom and equality (Shade, 1997). Blacks value group unity (Shade et al., 1997) and focus on justice and fairness (Locke, 1992). Caste-like minorities such as Blacks, Mexicans, and Puerto Ricans devote an enormous effort to fighting for political, social, and economic equality from the dominant group (Ogbu, 1983). Caste-like minority

(Grossman, 1998). Teachers and students developing positive interactive relationships can improve many discipline problems (Chappell & McCoy, 2003).

## *Teacher-Student Verbal and Nonverbal Behavior*

Education is a communication process that is not limited to transmitting knowledge but also involves interpersonal communication behaviors and nonverbal behaviors that are the major aspects of interpersonal relationships, which are critical in all learning situations (Victoria, 1970). The teaching-learning process is essentially a communication event (Knapp, 1971, p. 243) that includes verbal and nonverbal communication (Ikeda & Beebe, 1992). Teachers and students are verbal and nonverbal message senders and receivers (Parker & French, 1971). Developing respectful relationships with students requires considerable knowledge of their verbal and nonverbal communication styles (Brown, 2003).

Schools and Black student conflict develop from expectation differences related to communication styles (Gilbert & Gay, 1985). The general public fails to accept that Blacks have different communication norms and conventions by assuming that Blacks communicate using standards set by socially dominant Whites (Kochman, 1981). Whites' dispassionate and detached communication mode creates distrust among Blacks due to its similarity to Blacks who front which occurs when Blacks perceive there is a communication risk factor and chooses to remain silent in Black-White communication encounters. Most Black educational failure arises from the teachers' inability to understand how the students communicate (Gay & Abrahams, 1972). According to Brown (2003), "Urban educators must be aware of specific verbal and nonverbal communication styles that affect students' ability and motivation to engage in learning activities (p. 280).

## *Teacher-Student Verbal Behavior*

Black verbal communication styles can influence teacher-student classroom relationships. White Americans' unfamiliarity with the Black communication style results in a misunderstanding by the American mainstream (Corsini & Fogliasso, 1997).

According to Gay and Abrahams (1972):

> The majority of culture in the schools arises because of differences in the communication and interaction system. Lower-class Blacks in the United States do not communicate the same way other Americans do and that troubles us a good deal. It especially irritates those of us who have operated most of our lives on the assimilationist ideal – the melting pot set of expectations – and must include a great majority of teachers in this country. (p. 69)

Blacks not only debate the idea; they also debate the person while Whites debate the idea rather than the person debating the idea (Kochman, 1981). "Blacks often probe beyond a given statement to find out where a person is "coming from," in order to clarify the meaning and value of a particular behavior or attitude (Kochman, 1981, p. 23). Black students contrast White middle-class communication when they speak over others' voices and repeat the communication until they are responded to or until they have someone's attention (Gay & Abrahams, 1972). Patton et al. (1993) reported:

> Spontaneity in conversation is an acceptable component of [Black] communication, although others perceive interrupting another speaker in conversation as rude. Speaker and audience are often interchangeable as a [Black] listener will often "call out" or respond to a speaker. (p. 10)

Black communities accept the approach that their children use by interrupting others or speaking out of turn, which is an unacceptable school practice, and teachers view this behavior as disruptive and inappropriate (Hanna, 1988). Anglo Americans place a high value on allowing one person at a time to speak to indicate respect for an individual (Milburn, 2000).

Black children's socialization process includes achieving direction through indirection by saying one thing and doing another, which includes using metaphors and symbolism to approach issues in a roundabout manner (Gay, 1975). Blacks will tell European Americans what they want to hear, which may not be the truth, when pressured (Dace, 1994). Blacks verbally communicate by using a preponderance of words that denote action and unrestricted movement (Kochman, 1981) and by telling the truth or telling it like it is (Shade et al., 1997). Black communities view truth-telling or telling it-like-it-is verbal communication as courageous and honest, and a refusal to compromise integrity. Anglo European cultures view this communication as confrontational. Teachers find that attempts to communicate with difficult students may become strained, difficult, or awkward, and therefore such attempts can become impossible (Powell & Caseau, 2004).

Black students use several verbal techniques to discover a teacher's strengths and weaknesses in order to evaluate a teacher's racial attitudes and locate teachers' breaking points to help the students empower themselves in the situation between them and the teacher (Abrahams & Gay, 1972). Abrahams and Gay (1972) reported:

> If a [Black student] expects to rise to the position of a leader, he must know how to keep his cool. If he cannot respond to a [teachers challenge] without becoming frustrated and unnerved, he is not likely

to have the respect of others or remain a leader for long. (p. 205)

"When Blacks are working hard to keep it cool, it signals that the chasm between is getting wider, not smaller" (McCarty, 1981, p. 20). According to Gay (2000):

Black Students "gain the floor" or get participatory entry into conversations through personal assertiveness, the strength of the impulse to be involved, and persuasive power of the point they wish to make, rather than waiting for "authority" to grant permission. (p. 91)

In the classroom, Black students power play by loud talking or back-talking to make teachers lose their cool and get the last word in (Abrahams & Gay, 1972). Black students believe teachers show them respect by addressing them as Mr., Mrs., Sir, or Ma'am (Howard, 2001). Ignoring cultural differences between Blacks and Whites exists when attempting to understand Black and White communication failures (Kochman, 1981). Some Black students engage in verbal communicative activities that may inhibit positive teacher-student classroom relationships development as well as Hispanic students.

Hispanic students use specific language and speech patterns that may inhibit positive teacher-student relationship development. Puerto Ricans involved in the decision-making process may use rising intonation, qualifiers, questions, and hedges (Milburn, 2000). Puerto Ricans make decisions jointly where one person speaks and others join in and respond until the group makes a decision. Anglo Americans value one person speaking at a time to indicate respect for the individual. Puerto Ricans use indirectas, a form of speech, which is an indirect way of making something known. Morris (1981) reported:

> Indirectas are literally, indirect statements critical of others – insinuations, innuendo. They are disguised or purposely vague to any but the initiated, but clear in meaning to the ones who know the circumstance or the people involved. In form they do not give away either the person speaking or the person spoken of; they seem not to be barbed and directed to particulars, but they are meaningful in context. Anyone who is "in the know" does know how they are applied. (p. 102)

Hispanic students are more likely to participate in group consensus decisions rather than democratic processes (Grossman, 1995). According to Patton et al. (1993):

> Lively exchanges with interjections from all those involved are often found in Hispanic-American conversations, individuals do not need to wait for a pause to enter the discussion. Interruptions are

interpreted as eagerness, involvement, and

interest regarding the topic. (p. 11)

Most surveyed Hispanics and non-Hispanic participants agree Hispanics carry out multiple conversations without anyone being considered rude or discourteous (Grossman, 1995). Educators "assume that a child who is still and quiet has a better chance of learning than one who is noisy and active" (Parker & French, 1971, p. 277). White teachers may have difficulties in understanding minority students due to differences in dialect and language (Ornstein & Levine, 1990). Instructors can adapt to cultural differences by recognizing specific speaking pattern preferences and norms (Milburn, 2000).

Teacher-student classroom relationships include teacher verbal communication. Excellent communication skills ranks as one of the top three most important skills needed by teachers (Shanoski & Hranitz, 1991). Teachers have an opportunity to convey to students that the teachers care about such students by (a) talking to students at the end of the week regarding some shared topic or at the end of a unit, (b) talking to students when they are working on assignments, (c) commenting in a positive and affirming manner, and (d) talking to students at the beginning and end of the school week (Morganett, 1991).

Teachers can enhance students' feelings by talking to them. Some Black students believe that caring teachers yell and are strict, as long as the teacher does not overly use these strategies (Shanoski & Hranitz, 1991). Most American classrooms involve teacher-student exchanges in which teachers are clear, direct, explicit, and linear with their instruction and students are clear, direct, and explicit with their responses to questions (Powell & Caseau, 2004). Successful Hispanic students expect teachers to deliver information clearly, avoid showing any racial or ethnic discrimination, and care about their students (Cordeiro & Carspecken, 1993). Effective teachers vary voice, movement, and pace to refocus wandering student attention (Brophy, 1983). Teachers often respond to Hispanic students in louder and higher-pitched voices (Ortiz, 1988). Effective teachers minimize blameworthy behaviors by criticizing students less while ineffective teachers criticize students more (Brophy & Evertson, 1976; Good & Grouws, 1977; McDonald & Elias, 1976). Teachers are more likely to criticize poor work and poor answers (Brophy, 1981). Teachers who constantly correct students during reading assignments inhibit them from absorbing the meaning of the readings (Cummins, 1986). Most surveyed Hispanics and non-Hispanic participants disagree that educators should encourage students to work more independently rather than not provide students with approval and feedback (Grossman, 1998). Better teachers do not have nervous mannerisms in their speech when under pressure, and when under pressure, they remain relaxed so that the rhythm of their speech is unaffected (Anderson, Norton, & Nussbaum, 1981). Teachers who perceive students as high achievers tend to use more words and speak in a tone that is more positive to these students (Bates, 1976). Teachers who engage students one on one in casual conversation before class begins lose most of the students' interest after 20 minutes (Chappell & McCoy, 2003).

Teachers use praise to engage students in the learning process. Verbal encouragement by teachers increases student participation and desired behavior (Keith, Tornatzky, & Pettigrew, 1974). Praise is an effective reinforcement that provides encouragement to students and is reinforcement for behavior performance improvement (Hughes, 1973; O'Leary & O'Leary, 1977; Rosenshine,

1976). Praise is an effective reinforcement that helps to build student self-esteem (Brophy, 1981).

Teachers are more likely to praise good answers and good work rather than poor answers or poor work (Brophy, 1981). Teachers praise Hispanic students less and give them less feedback for answering questions correctly as well as appropriate performances (Grossman, 1998). Most surveyed Hispanics and non-Hispanic participants agree educators should praise Hispanic students for individual achievement as well as cooperative behavior. A little more than half of surveyed Hispanics and non-Hispanic participants agree educators should use rewards such as praise, hugs, pats on the back, and other personal rewards for Hispanics rather than checks, gold stars, sweets, and toys. Mexican American mothers with higher education and income levels use praise and inquiry to teach their children while less educated Mexican American mothers with lower incomes use more modeling to teach their children (Laosa, 1980). Black gifted achievers receive less attention, are least praised, and most criticized in a classroom, even when compared to their nonachieving and nongifted Black counterparts (Rubovits & Maehr, 1973). Black students receive less attention, and praise, and receive more criticism when compared to nongifted Blacks while the same teachers treat gifted Whites more positively than nongifted Whites. Black children react more favorably to praise while White children react more to reproof (Hurlock, 1924).

Teachers give more praise and less criticism to opposite race children (Brown, Payne, Lankewich, & Cornell, 1970). In classes where the teacher and students are not of the same race, praise is significantly increased while classes where the teacher and student have the same race, praise is significantly decreased. However, White teachers were judged more pleased with praising White students rather than praising Black students (Feldman, 1976), and White females enrolled in a child development course for perspective elementary school teachers who taught a lesson for a group of fourth-, seventh-, and eighth-grade students praised Black students less (Rubovits & Maehr, 1973). Some students believe praise is a punishment (Brophy, 1981). Teachers should encourage and praise students for doing their best, regardless of their work when compared to other students (Ashmore & Project M.E.D.I.A, 1984).

Praise can reduce motivation if used when students are performing the desired behavior (Brophy, 1981). Teachers praise students more when students are having trouble mastering the material even though they are working hard or when the students display unacceptable disruptive behavior rather than praise students who are quiet, comforting, well-adjusted, and high achieving (Evertson, Anderson, Anderson, & Brophy, 1980; Silberman, 1969). Teachers perceive students whom the teachers wish to remove from their classrooms as low achievers, and these students alienate teachers by continual defiance and disobedience (Brophy & Good, 1974; Good & Brophy, 1972; Willis & Brophy, 1974), which causes teachers to respond with frequent praise to make up for negative behavior (Silberman, 1969). However, students whom teachers believe are a joy to teach receive more praise and less criticism in the classroom when compared to other students (Good & Brophy, 1972). Students are able to get teachers to praise them by bringing completed assignments to teachers and exhibiting qualities such as confidence, sociability, and extroversion (Brophy, Evertson, Anderson, Baum, & Crawford, 1976). Students reward teachers for their praise by smiling and beaming positively (Brophy, 1981). Philosophical objections to praise result from teachers who desire to develop egalitarian relationships with their students and teachers who want to develop independent thinking in their students so that students are less dependent on the teacher. Praise is an effective reinforcement that provides encouragement to students, helps to build student self-esteem, and helps to build close teacher-student classroom relationships (Brophy, 1981).

Humor is a positive way to promote positive teacher-student classroom relationships (Powell & Caseau, 2004). Humor can build and strengthen teacher-student relationships, especially on the individual level (Rareshide, 1993). Humor is used to (a) connect the speaker with the audience, such as the teacher and the student (Meyer, 2000; Rareshide, 1993), (b) clarify a view or idea (Meyer, 2000), (c) level criticisms so the speaker can continue to identify with the audience to include reinforcing class rules and expectations for normative behaviors, and (d) contrast the views of others with themselves, which teachers use as sarcasm or teasing. Humor increases the connection between the teacher and the student when it reduces tensions between the teacher and the student (Powell & Caseau, 2004; Rareshide, 1993) and reveals that the teacher is also human (Powell & Caseau, 2004). Humor results from teachers, who attempt to connect to students personally, stimulate the learning experience, use humor as an alternative to authoritarian discipline, and encourage risk-taking and higher-level thinking (Goor, 1989). Humor is effective for students who are not interested or motivated in the instructional topic (Vance, 1987). Humor can motivate students who are bored, stressed, or have negative attitudes toward school (Colwell & Wigle, 1984) and add meaning to the instructional topic (Vance, 1987). Teachers believe (a) humor shows students teachers are human and can make mistakes, (b) humor should never embarrass, ridicule, or harm the student, and (c) purposeless humor can result in student misbehavior and waste valuable instructional time (Rareshide, 1993).

Humor helps students learn when used effectively and appropriately (Rareshide, 1993). In classrooms where teachers encourage laughter, students learn and retain more information (Chenfeld, 1990). Humor is ineffective when students are already motivated (Vance, 1987). Teachers must use humor naturally, or else it can backfire (Bryant & Zillman, 1988). Teachers who use irrelevant jokes and humor reduce instructional time (Sullivan, 1992). Teachers can damage students' self-esteem by joking about a student's name. Mexican Americans use jokes and humor to avoid disagreements (Shade et al., 1997). Blacks and

Mexican Americans verbally communicate by using jokes and humor.

Teachers are more likely to use humor with mature students (Rareshide, 1993). Teachers usually incorporate some type of humor in their instruction with students who will respond enthusiastically. Teachers develop similarity and identification with students when students respond positively to jokes and stories (Timmerman, 1995). Teachers lower their personal status and raise student status by making fun of themselves (Powell & Caseau, 2004). Middle-school teachers can use humor to build rapport, empower learners, promote problem solving, create interest, enhance student self-esteem, and emphasize socialization (Pollack & Freda, 1997). Most interviewed high school students removed from class for behavioral challenges indicate positive teacher characteristics include a sense of humor (Pomery, 1999). Humor results from the realization that a mistake was made that is not bad or harmful (Shibles, 1978).

However, sarcasm can damage teacher-student relationships (Kryston, Smith, Collins, Hamilton, 1986). Children believe sarcastic messages are negative (Blanck & Rosenthal, 1982). Teachers believe sarcasm may psychologically damage children (Sava, 2002). According to Bryant and Zillman (1988), sarcasm and ridicule "may serve a corrective function, the long-term consequence of diminished esteem in the eyes of students may make the immediate gains in terms of behavioral correction not worth the costs" (p. 72). Interviews with high school students removed for behavioral challenges indicate antagonistic and humiliating teacher behaviors include sarcastic responses (Pomery, 1999). Teachers believe students have greater understanding of vocal contradictions and sarcasm as grade level increases (Anderson, Anderson,

Murphy, & Wendt-Wasco, 1986). Older children are better at decoding discrepant nonverbal cues when they are attached to sarcastic messages (Blanck & Rosenthal, 1982). Criticism decreases student performance (Brophy & Evertson, 1974; Rosenshine, 1976).

Teacher sarcasm can devastate the positive teacher-student classroom relationship process. Teachers need to develop strategies that will develop positive teacher-student classroom relationships. Teachers can reveal something regarding themselves to begin this process.

Effective teacher-student interactions involve teachers revealing something regarding themselves that students do not know about their teachers (Cooper & Simmonds, 1999). This influences the relationship between the teacher and the student, and eventually influences how the students feel regarding the content (Powell & Caseau, 2004). Students respond to teachers who are personable and social, and make learning fun and relevant (Heller & Scottile, 1996). Self-disclosure is likely to have a positive impact when used by teachers to illustrate a concept, reveal a struggle, or show difficulty learning a concept (Powell & Caseau, 2004). Good teachers are more likely to engage in disclosive statements that reflect concern for students while poor teachers disclosive statements are evaluative or reflect a negative outlook.

Interviewed teachers, students, and administrators believe teachers who develop positive relationships with students have the ability to make enough self-disclosures that students perceive their teachers as genuine, place an emphasis on mutual respect, and find the right balance between being firm, friendly, and fair (Vitto, 2003). Blacks build trust slowly with European Americans, especially after encountering negative stereotyping and discrimination (Collier & Powell, 1990). When dominant culture persons deny or diminish information regarding Blacks or misrepresent their experiences, then Blacks will not self-disclose (Dace, 1994). European Americans are disappointed when Blacks do not trust them and disclose information early in a relationship. According to Powell and Caseau (2004), "students from Euro-American backgrounds probably disclose the most in class. Students from high-context cultures are less likely to engage in self-disclosure. Native Americans, Asians, and Latinos are less likely to engage in self-disclosure or feel that it is appropriate" (p. 123). Blacks stop self-disclosing and hesitate to self-disclose when others are partially committed to listening and understanding (Gates, 1998). When European Americans consistently demonstrate trustworthiness, then Blacks will truthfully self-disclose (Collier & Powell, 1990; Dace, 1994; Orbe, 1994). Self-disclosure may require that teachers and students engage in a question and answer communication process.

Teacher questioning techniques can influence teacher-student classroom relationships. When teachers ask respectful questions, students feel they are in a trusting environment that makes them sense that they are safe (Wassermann, 1992). Questions that humiliate students diminish student confidence. Teachers who ask trick questions respond in an arrogant or derogatory manner when students do not respond. Teachers who ask questions to boost their egos will not gain students' respect or admiration. Stupid questions are insulting and can cause anger and frustration. Black students do not appreciate when teachers ask direct personal questions (Patton et al., 1993).

Black and Hispanic students have cultural experiences that can impede classroom question-and-answer sessions. Cultural conflicts between the teacher and Black students may surface because of basic question-and-answer sessions because question-and-answer sessions develop when an adult is angry with them (Gay & Abrahams, 1972). Blacks learn that question-and-answer sessions result when an adult is angry with them, and this process may inhibit students from classroom involvement (Bennett, 1997). Mexican American students respond only when spoken to, initiate only to ask academic questions, and fail to volunteer responses or make other types of questions or comments in the regular classroom (McClure, 1978). Mexican American students are more likely to direct comments and questions to teachers for guidance (McClure, 1978) and receive fewer product questions and affirmation following correct answers (Buriel, 1983) when compared to Anglo American students. Mexican American children's achievement is positively correlated to teacher affirmation after a correct answer. Most surveyed Hispanics and a little fewer than half non-Hispanic participants agree that Hispanic students are reluctant to participate in classroom discussions of controversial topics and issues (Grossman, 1998). A little more than half of surveyed Hispanics and non-Hispanic participants agree that teachers should allow Hispanic students to assist each other when called on to answer questions in the classroom.

Educators who react negatively to student call response behaviors may strain the relationship between the teacher and the student (Obidah & Manheim Teel, 2001). The Black verbal response pattern is usually unnoticed by Whites (Asante & Davis, 1985). Black students may request a speaker, such as a teacher, to repeat the information several times because of disbelief or surprise or as a compliment to the speaker (Abrahams & Gay, 1972). Denying a Black student's request for assistance and request to repeat information that results from the student's inability to handle Standard English may cause complete withdrawal from the educational process. Blacks receive less verbal contact indicating that their responses are correct, acceptable, or appropriate from White teachers when compared to White students (Byalick & Bershoff, 1974). Hispanics are often ignored or given less time to respond to teachers' questions (Ortiz, 1988). Teachers often ignore Hispanic children, and if teachers call on Hispanic children, the teachers implement less wait time for responses when compared with other children and call on them using louder and higher-pitched voices, which indicate that the teachers are irritated. A little more than half of surveyed Hispanics and non-Hispanic participants agree Hispanic students may not volunteer answers or pretend not to know the correct answer because of their belief that it is bad manners to try to excel over others

(Grossman, 1998). Students increase involvement in classroom discussions when teachers respond to wrong answers by working with the student instead of rejecting the answer outright (Shirley, 2003). Black and Hispanic student verbal classroom behaviors can affect teacher-student classroom relationship development.

Cultural differences can affect teacher-student classroom relationships when debates occur in the classroom. Blacks and Whites ignore communication failures because Blacks and Whites assume they are communicating with the standards set by socially dominant Whites (Kochman, 1981). For Whites, the purpose of an argument is to ventilate anger and hostility. "Blacks distinguish between an argument used to debate a difference of opinion and an argument used to ventilate anger and hostility" (Kochman, 1981, p.18). Whites misinterpret Black intentions to solve a disagreement and do not believe Blacks who want to solve a disagreement. "A request from a Black person to a white person may be encountered as a demand" (Asante & Davis, 1985, p. 91). Blacks communicate in debates by becoming high-keyed, animated, interpersonal, and confrontational while middle-class Whites communicate in debates by becoming low-keyed, dispassionate, impersonal, and non-challenging (Kochman, 1981). Most surveyed Hispanics and a little less than half non-Hispanic participants agree Hispanic students may be uncomfortable with debating issues in public (Grossman, 1998). Most surveyed Hispanics and non-Hispanic participants agree educators should explain to Hispanic students that debating in the classroom is appropriate and not considered impolite or improper. The difference in Black and Hispanic, and White debating behavior can cause classroom argument between minority students and White teachers.

Some in-class arguments between teachers and Black students are a product of the Blacks system of language socialization that involves students talking, which gets others in the group to listen and respond (Gay & Abrahams, 1972). One of the most common student classroom infractions is talking (Wragg, 1995). Black students are inclined to talk back when motivated by what a teacher says (Gay, 1975). Black students may become so impressed with the speaker, such as a teacher, that students will want to hear the speaker again due to an interest in how it was said (Abrahams & Gay, 1972). Black students also exhibit affective classroom behavior that can influence positive teacher-student classroom relationships. Urban Black students want to create the appropriate mood and setting before beginning to work on a task by asking the teacher to repeat the directions (Gilbert & Gay, 1985). Blacks will argue for recognition of unsuccessful efforts toward completing a task. Many teachers do not expect Black students to interrupt the class by talking to their neighbors and speak without raising their hands (Shade, 1994). Educators assume quiet students are successful and receive rewards for making teaching an easier task (Parker & French, 1971). Teachers respond to students talking in the classroom without permission by ordering, reprimanding, involving students in work, and naming the student (Wragg, 1995). When a teacher yells, uses harsh words, shames, degrades, or embarrasses a student, such behavior influences all students (Vitto, 2003). Most surveyed Hispanics and a little less than half non-Hispanic participants agree, educators should be indirect rather than direct and frank, and respectful rather than disrespectful when reprimanding or disciplining Hispanic students (Grossman, 1995). Teachers who use coercion, an attempt to manage students by applying sanctions such as detention, suspension, and corporal punishment, are ineffective when working with resistant students (Glasser, 1990). Resistant students view this as the boss using coercion and become the teacher's adversaries.

Most teachers react to students as authoritarians when involved in conflict situations (Spector, 1955). Teachers who use excessive authority may psychologically damage children (Sava, 2002). When working with difficult students, most teachers focus their conversations on what the students are lacking by coercing, reminding, or lecturing the students on what they should be doing, which does not build positive relationships and can make matters worse (Vitto, 2003).

Demanding that students submit to teacher authority may result in increased student disruption, therefore decreasing time spent in the learning process (Clegg & Megson, 1968; Heal, 1978; Hoy, 1968; Rutter, Maughan,

Mortimore, Ouston, & Smith, 1979; Wlodkoski, 1982). Most surveyed Hispanics and a little less than half non-Hispanic participants agree that when educators speak to Hispanic students in an authoritarian manner, Hispanic students may feel insulted, angry, or resentful, and lose a desire to cooperate or conform as well as lose respect for the educator (Grossman, 1995). Students whom teachers want removed from class are more likely to receive criticism from the teacher when seeking individual assistance and for classroom behavior and work (Good & Brophy, 1972). Less than half of surveyed non-Hispanics agree that Hispanic parents discipline or criticize their children by speaking politely and indirectly while educators in the United States are more gruff and direct with students (Grossman, 1995). Some teachers develop positive teacher-student relationships when they are managing inappropriate student behavior (Vitto, 2003).

***Teacher-Student Nonverbal Behavior***

Nonverbal classroom communication is more important than verbal classroom behavior (Keith et al., 1974). Nonverbal communication contributes significantly to communicative interpersonal interactions when compared to verbal communication (Birdwhistell, 1970; Mehrabian, 1968). Nonverbal communication has greater significance than verbal communication that results from nonverbal communication, having a greater impact (a) in determining interpersonal context meaning, (b) when accurately determining feelings and emotions, (c) when revealing meanings and intentions that are deception and distortion free, (d) when attaining high-quality communications that represent a much more effective communication medium, and (e) represent a more suitable means of communication when compared to verbal communication (Leathers, 1997). According to Richmond (2002):

> The primary function of teachers' nonverbal behavior in the classroom is to improve affect or liking for the subject matter, teacher, and class and to increase the desire to learn more about the subject matter. One step toward this is the development of a positive affective relationship between the student and the teacher. When the teacher improves affect through effective nonverbal behavior, then the students are more likely to listen more, learn more, and have a more positive attitude about the school. (p. 70)

Students who perceive that teachers feel favorable toward them demonstrate desired classroom behaviors (Davidson & Lang, 1960). Students are more likely to complete assignments in classes that they feel accepted by the teacher (Morganett, 1991).

Nonverbal communication includes three interacting systems, the visual, auditory, and invisible communication systems (Leathers, 1997). Auditory communication involves loudness, pitch, rate, duration, quality, regularity, articulation, pronunciation, and pitch. Visual communication is the most important nonverbal communication system, and includes kinesthetic, proxemic, and artifactual subsystems. Kinesthetic communication includes facial expression, eye behaviors, gestures, and posture. Proxemic communication involves the use of space, distance, and territory for communication purposes. Artifactual communication involves facial and bodily appearances and the options that communicators use to alter their appearance. Individuals who nonverbally communicate in a manner consistent with a culture are perceived as more interpersonally attractive by members of that culture (Dew & Ward, 1993). Teachers who identify, analyze, and modify, if necessary, their nonverbal behavior improve their effectiveness. Teachers can learn to become effective by attending and completing a teacher preparation programs offered at colleges.

Colleges teach teachers to ensure there is a distance between themselves and the students so the teacher can maintain discipline in the classroom (Valverde, 2006). European Americans are more likely to have close social distance with Mexican Americans when compared to Blacks (Burmal, 1970) and prefer to keep their personal space at arm's length (Patton et al., 1993). Hispanic Americans stand close to or side by side instead of face-to-face when talking to another person (Grossman, 1995; Patton et al., 1993). Hispanic Americans stand 6 to 8 inches within an arm's length when talking to another person

(Patton et al., 1993). Latinos interact at a close distance and frequently touch one another (Baxter, 1970; Shuter, 1976). Latino Americans prefer closer standing distances when compared to North Americans (Leathers, 1997). Most surveyed Hispanics and non-Hispanic participants agree that Hispanics feel rejected when people back away from them (Grossman, 1995). Blacks prefer closer social distance (Bauer, 1973; Hall, 1966; Liebman, 1970; Shade, 1997) when compared to Mexican Americans (Baxter, 1970; Shade, 1997). Blacks are more likely to touch each other in a conversation when compared to Whites (Willis, 1966). Individuals who perceive a proximity violator as someone who will provide them with negative rewards will react negatively when the proximity violator moves closer (Leathers, 1997). Maintaining the appropriate or comfortable proximity is associated with a positive effect, friendship, and attraction.

Teachers who are sensitive to various cultures will learn about student interaction patterns that may affect student classroom participation (Leiding, 2006). Preventing misbehavior and maintaining a positive classroom climate require three to five positive interactions with students to every one negative interaction (Sprick, Garrison, & Howard, 1998). Interaction distances increase as children grow older (Lerner, Karabeneck, & Meisels, 1975; Tennis & Dabbs, 1975). Interaction space decreases as liking or acquaintance between individuals in a dyad increases (Guardo, 1969; Guardo & Meisels, 1971; Meisals & Guardo, 1969). Adolescents interact at closer distances than adults but farther distances than children (Baxter, 1970).

Schools and Black students' conflict develops from expectation differences related to interaction styles (Gilbert & Gay, 1985). Black children in grades one to four tend to stand closer for communication purposes when compared to other ethnic groups (Aiello & Jones, 1971; Duncan, 1978; Jones & Aiello, 1973). White Americans believe Blacks should interact with them by acknowledging their cultural identity, being socially polite and friendly, and supporting their arguments while Mexican Americans should interact with them by being socially polite, which includes speaking proper English, showing concern for the other individual, and being assertive and friendly (Colier, 1988). Black Americans believe Whites should interact with them by being polite to the other as an individual, supporting their arguments and making them relevant, and being assertive. Mexican Americans believe Whites should interact with them by being socially polite, showing concern for the individual, acknowledging their cultural identity, being friendly, staying on topic, and showing openness. Black and White teachers provide Black male students with more interactions such as criticism, question-

and-response nonacceptance, and behavior-controlling questions (Hillman & Davenport, 1978). Students can assess their academic and social capabilities from classroom interactions (Stanworth, 1983). The relationship between classroom interactions and achievement depends upon lesson type, student ability, and the emotional climate of the classroom (Brophy & Good, 1986; Soar, 1977; Soar & Soar, 1979). Teachers and students may decrease their interaction distance when they feel comfortable with each other, which may influence how teachers assign students seating arrangement within the classroom.

Teachers assign seating for disruptive students first and then assign students who do not have disruptive behavior to sit next to the disruptive students (Schwebel & Cherlin, 1972). Disruptive students may interpret seat assignments at the front of the classroom as resulting from a special relationship with the teacher (Schwebel &

Cherlin, 1972). Insecure and anxious teachers represent their authority by establishing a territory around their desk (Schusler, 1971). Even though teachers have the authority to assign students seating patterns they are still required to facilitate a learning environment that is conducive to high student achievement.

Teachers are required to present themselves as friends and facilitators of learning rather than purveyors of knowledge (Schusler, 1971). Teachers create a warmer classroom climate for students the teachers have high expectations of by smiling (Chaikin, Gillen, Derlega, Heinen, & Wilson, 1978; Millard & Stimpson, 1980). Effective teachers exhibit enthusiasm by facial expressions (Murray, 1983; Nussbaum, 1992; Weimer, 1990), which positively influences student attitudes and student perceptions of teachers (Chaikin et al., 1978; Millard & Stimpson, 1980). Cognitive learning increases when teachers smile at the class (Gorham, 1988). Teachers who smile are perceived as friendly while a frowning teacher is perceived as mean or grumpy (Powell & Caseau, 2004). Frowns from teachers who conduct demanding lessons with high-ability students may indicate a belief that students are capable of excellence while the same frown may indicate low expectations and impatience when the teachers conduct a remedial lesson with slow students (Weinstein, 1983).

Individuals use nonverbal cues to indicate a disliking for another individual by unpleasant facial expressions (Leathers, 1997). "Negative emotions are more acceptable when indicated by facial expression in the [Black] culture" (Patton et al., 1993, p. 9). Blacks have a high sensitivity to facial expressions (Shade et al., 1997), which provides them with superior facial expression and other emotion evaluation skills when compared to other ethnic groups (Shade, 1983). Blacks interpret communication meaning by interpreting facial gestures (Pasteur & Toldson, 1982). Black females pay closer attention to male facial expressions rather than physical characteristics when compared to White females (Hirschberg, Jones, & Haggerty, 1978). Teachers should consider Black facial expression evaluation techniques when conveying approval or disapproval to students.

Teacher facial expressions can convey approval or disapproval to students (Keith et al., 1974). Black students receive less positive facial attention from White teachers when compared to White students (Byalick & Bershoff, 1974). Black and White teachers demonstrate positive facial expressions toward students of their own culture when compared to students from a different culture (Feldman & Donohue, 1978). Frequent smiles are one of many positive signals used in junior and senior high school (Koch, 1971).

Individuals can also use facial expressions such as eye contact to convey liking for another individual. Individuals use nonverbal cues to indicate a liking for another individual by initiating and maintaining eye contact (Leathers, 1997). Whites believe maintaining eye contact in face-to-face communication is most desirable (Asante & Davis, 1985). White American employees and employers believe maintaining eye contact communicates trustworthiness, masculinity, sincerity, and directedness and conclude when Black employees fail to maintain eye contact that the Black employees have something to hide. European Americans view looking away or looking downward as a sign of disinterest, shyness, or disrespect (Patton et al., 1993).

Within Black culture, avoiding eye contact is a sign of disrespect (Johnson, 1971). Some Black parents teach their children that looking an adult in the eye is a sign of disrespect while White children learn to do the opposite (Byers & Byers, 1972). When reprimanding Black children, they tend not to look at the teacher as a sign of respect (Patton et al., 1993). Blacks are less likely to maintain eye contact with persons in a position of authority (Asante & Davis, 1985), and Black children increase eye contact as they begin to trust the teacher (Patton et al., 1993). Black students who avert their eyes and verbally express themselves may be just as attentive as White students who gaze directly at the speaker (Feldman, 1985). Students may avoid teacher eye contact when they do not want to be called on or do not know the answer and respond by busily taking notes, rearranging books and papers, and fropping their pencils (Knapp, 1971). Black adults gaze at others when talking to indicate interest (Patton et al., 1993). Blacks often "give the eye" as a displeasure indication related to negative feelings. Black eye contact behavior can result in increasing eye contact period when interacting with persons.

Extended eye contact can indicate aggressive anxiety in others (Knapp, 1971). Hispanic students in mainstream classrooms address and respond to teachers clearly, concisely, and require that the teacher look at them (Ortiz, 1988). Hispanic students in bilingual classrooms may lower their heads, look away, and giggle. Hispanic Americans view prolonged eye contact as disrespectful (Patton et al., 1993). Hispanic American children lower their eyes when reprimanded. Latino Americans believe disagreement expressions and eye contact with senior citizens is rude (Gates, 1998).

Eye contact behavior can influence teacher-student classroom relationships. Teachers must also consider how other nonverbal behavior can promote positive teacher-student classroom relationships. Teacher and student listening behavior can influence teacher-student classroom relationships.

Teachers can enhance students' feelings by listening to them (Morganett, 1991). Blacks indicate they are listening by nodding their heads (Erickson, 1979; Feldman, 1985; Shade et al., 1997). In the United States, a head nod signifies agreement (Leathers, 1997). In White culture, a perpendicular nod during a conversation indicates an agreement, acceptance, or understanding (Asante & Davis, 1985). In the Black culture, a perpendicular nod during a conversation indicates a conversational catalyst, not an agreement, acceptance, or understanding. Blacks indicate they are listening by making short sounds (Feldman, 1985;

Shade et al., 1997), and verbally respond (Erickson, 1979) to indicate that they are listening. Blacks accept interrupting others or speaking-out-of-turn communicative approach as valued and an indication that the individual is listening, comprehending, and has anticipated the point being made (Shade, 1994). "A Black child may be listening intently, yet to a [W]hite person he gives the appearance of distraction, often because of a different habit of directing his gaze" (Gay & Abrahams, 1972, p. 77). When Black children are thinking of a response, they look away when listening (Patton et al., 1993).

Teachers may unknowingly provide inconsistent educational goals that affect students by not considering how they relate to students (Schwebel & Cherlin, 1972). Relating to student may require teachers to consider other dynamics that involve teacher-student nonverbal behavior.

Teachers may need to consider how physical contact can influence teacher-student classroom relationships.

Researchers report teachers can relate to students by physical contact. Many teachers do not expect Black students to need a great deal of physical contact (Shade, 1994). "If an individual such as a teacher touches an African American child, it then becomes acceptable for the child to touch the teacher" (Patton et al., 1993, p. 6). Touching school-aged Blacks on the shoulder, back, arms, or hand is usually reserved for close, intimate relationships with adults. Black students receive less positive physical contact from White teachers when compared to White students (Byalick & Bersoff, 1974). Hispanic Americans pat friends or family on the back or arm when talking (Patton et al., 1993). Most surveyed Hispanics and non-Hispanic participants agree educators should express Hispanic student approval and acceptance by using physical contact (Grossman, 1995). Teachers believe touching between students and teachers decreases as the grade level increases (Anderson et al., 1986).

Touching between teachers and students can influence classroom relationship development between teachers and students. Teachers and student also exhibit physical behavior regarding their posture. Teacher student posture behavior and posture behavior interpretation can influence teacher-student classroom relationships.

Individuals use nonverbal cues to indicate a disliking for another individual by incongruent postures (Leathers, 1997). Blacks' conversing in a relaxed posture is common (Patton et al., 1993). However, a relaxed listening stance may indicate that the listener is tuning out the speaker. Turning away during conversation may also indicate respect and interest or a discussion of personal issues. Cognitive learning increases when teachers have a relaxed body position (Gorham, 1988). Better teachers are more relaxed (Anderson et al., 1981). Deciphering posture influence requires evaluating nonverbal behavior.

Nonverbal behavior also includes teacher-student physical attributes. Physical attributes can influence teacher-student classroom relationships. "In school settings, teachers seem to expect physically attractive children to be more successful, academically and socially" (Leathers, 1997, p. 144). Because of this expectation, a physically attractive child often becomes the teacher's pet (Leathers, 1997). Students in secondary school settings perceive that dress affects intelligence and academic potential. Taller males and females are perceived by children as stronger when compared to their counterparts.

Teacher physical characteristics can influence teacher-student classroom relationships. Teachers have the authority to arrange the physical layout for their classrooms. Teachers can increase student motivation by decorating the classroom in a way that is appealing to students (Leathers, 1997). According to Morganett (1991), students who lack motivation attain unsatisfactory levels of learning and become classroom management problems. Enhancing student motivation to develop positive teacher-student relationships requires teachers to prepare physically appealing environments.

# *Teacher-Student Racial Differences*

Racial differences between teachers and students influence positive teacher-student classroom relationship development. Teacher-student conflicts result from a difference in desires, and even though this difference may be reduced, it remains in schools (Waller, 1932). According to Collier and Powell (1990), "cultural background affects attitudes, beliefs, and values about education, ideas about how classes ought to be conducted, how students and teachers ought to interact, and what types of relationships are appropriate for students and teachers" (p. 334). The classroom conflict between teachers and students results from the different cultural contexts that students and teachers bring to the classroom (Hall, 1989; McDermott, 1977).

Some minorities believe they cannot trust White institutions (Ogbu, 1992). Adolescents may develop oppositional social identities that are contrary to the social expectations of mainstream society when they experience racism and respond with anger and rebellion (Comer, 1976; Ogbu, 1988). Black students are convinced that White teachers are racist and prejudiced (Gay & Abrahams, 1972) and reject White teachers' authority due to their experience with racism, and Black students who reach school develop a sharp distinction between acting Black and acting White (Ogbu, 1987). According to Howard (2001), Black students frequently find themselves in classrooms where their culture, racial, and linguistic identities are under constant attack that manifests as a multitude of disciplinary actions, suspensions, and expulsions. "There is also a great deal of prejudice against non-English speaking students" (Grossman, 1998, p. 12). Minority students are more likely to encounter teacher behavior that impedes their progress when compared to White students (Cooper et al., 1977; Datta et al., 1968; Dornbusch et al., 1975; Rubovits & Maehr, 1973).

Cultural racism results from the dominant or more powerful group defining cultural values and value characteristics (Twenge & Croker, 2002). Anti-Black prejudice in America has historical roots in slavery, carpetbagging, and the failure to reconstruct the South after the Civil War (Allport, 1954). The army set the stage for labeling Blacks as inferior by using the Alpha and Beta test that contained a number of visual information processing tasks that Blacks are not proficient at (Shade, 1997). American societal beliefs that posit Blacks as inferior to European Americans results in Blacks developing psycho-behavioral modalities such as self-hatred, over-identification with those in power, anxiety, hostility, aggression, and a general inadequate development of the motivational, cognitive, and intellectual skills necessary to survive American society (Ogbu, 1978). Burmal (1970) posits:

> Anglo-Americans believe that they are justified in withholding equal access to the rewards of full acceptance as long as Mexicans remain "different", particularly they interpret the differences as evidence of inferiority. Mexicans on the other hand, while not always certain that they are inferior, clearly want equal opportunity and full acceptance now, not in the some dim future, and they do not believe that their differences from Anglo-Americans offer any justification for the denial of opportunity and acceptance. (p. 393)

Many Anglo Americans believe Mexican Americans are inferior (Burmal, 1970). Recent actions such as states declaring English as the official language send a clear message to Hispanics that persons with linguistic and cultural differences cannot be tolerated (Shade, 1997). Cultural background affects what types of relationships are appropriate for teachers and students (Collier & Powell, 1990).

# *Teacher-Student Relationships*

The ideal teacher-student relationship includes dialogue and "mutually respectful treatment between individuals in the working relationship" (Pomery, 1999, p. 480). Positive relationships at schools and in the classroom are in many ways the prerequisites for effective learning and behavior (Pianta, 1999). Students and teachers who are warm, compassionate, and friendly toward one another in the classroom have the potential to improve instruction and learning (Kearney, 1984). Teachers can build positive teacher-student classroom relationships. The keys to positive relationships with students are (a) checking student knowledge by asking students what they already know, (b) providing students time to explore and discover, (c) celebrating student accomplishments, (d) respecting students, which includes expecting students to have wisdom, and (e) exploring how they view things and discussing differences (Vitto, 2003). Teachers develop positive relationships with students by engaging them in personal and meaningful dialogue that includes personal and nonacademic issues such as student interests, goals, aspirations, likes and dislikes, family, and culture.

Teachers practice developing positive relationships with students by using the first few or last few minutes of class time, between classes, tutorials, lunchtime, individual conferencing during independent work, after-school time, and sporting events (Vitto, 2003). According to Brown (1999), effective urban teaching involves developing respectful relationships. "The best urban teachers show warmth and affection to their students and give priority to the development of their relationships with students as an avenue to student growth" (Gordon, 1999, p. 305). Powell and Caseau (2004) concluded that teachers develop positive teacher-student classroom relationships in four stages. First, teachers and students develop relationships by initiation that begins the moment students walk into the classroom. During this stage, teachers start to form impressions that may be difficult to change, and students develop expectations regarding teachers. The second stage for teacher-student relationship development is experimenting. During this stage, teachers begin to collect information about the students that may influence future instructional strategies. Students experiment with the teacher by trying to sort out teacher dislikes and likes, classroom instructional and disciplinary boundaries, and teacher grading biases. Teachers and students find ways to manage their relationship with one another. The third stage for teacher-student relationship development is intensifying. During this stage, teachers and students make communication choices based on individual rather than stereotypical roles. Teachers begin to communicate care for students and circumstances that will enhance or constrain learning. The fourth stage for teacher-student relationship development is differentiating. During this stage, teachers and students learn about each other. "The negative effect accompanying this stage influences motivation and willingness to learn. Students avoid the teacher, and the teacher avoids the students: as a consequence, learning is compromised" (Powell & Caseau, 2004, p. 115).

Good teacher-student relationships include teachers communicating to students that they care about them (Morganett, 1991). Teachers who are caring, friendly, helpful, understanding, and dependable foster supportive relationships with their students (Goodenow, 1993; Rosenfield & Richman, 1999; Skinner & Belmount, 1993). Kohn (1996) concludes,

> Caring teachers' converse with students in a distinctive way: they think about how what they say sounds from the students' point of view. They respond authentically and respectfully rather than giving patronizing pats on the head (or otherwise slathering them with "positive reinforcement." They explain what they are up to and give reasons for their requests. (p. 112)

Teachers have an opportunity to converse with students who they care about by talking to students when school events interrupt normal activities (Morganett, 1991). Black students prefer warm and supportive teachers (St. John, 1971) and believe that teachers create an optimum learning environment when they care about and bond with their students (Howard, 2001).

Developing positive relationships with students provides benefits for schools, teachers, and students.

Having positive and caring relationships in schools increases resilience and protects children from academic failure, mental illness, drug and alcohol abuse, and destructive behavior and violence (Resnick et al., 1997). Long-term teacher-student relationships result in increased teacher job satisfaction (Burke, 1996). Teachers who have positive feelings toward their students are more likely to have students reciprocate those positive feelings (Plax, Kearney, McCroskey, & Richmond, 1986). Teachers who develop positive and personal relationships with students may prevent psychological development problems in their students (Vitto, 2003). Students are more willing to develop positive relationships with teachers who tend to form close friendships with their students (Grossack, 1955).

Positive teacher-student relationships include the absence of negative interactions (Vitto, 2003). Negative criticism, embarrassment, and humiliation are the most frequent acts that damage teacher-student relationships (Sava, 2002). The barriers to developing positive relationships with students also include (a) assuming how a student responds, thinks, and feels, (b) not allowing students to discover their own explanations and solutions, (c) bossing or telling a student what needs to be done and how it should be done, (d) criticizing students by pointing out what the students did not do right, and (e) pointing out to students that they should behave, think, and feel as adults (Vitto, 2003). Effective teaching techniques may lose some of their impact when positive teacher-student relationships are lacking (Pianta, 1999).

Quality teacher-student interactions are one of the most important variables that influence student achievement in the classroom (Norton & Dobson, 1976). "Because teacher-student interactions are at the very heart of the educational process, it is to be expected that they should have an important bearing on students' achievement" (Buriel, 1983, p. 890). Researchers report teacher-student interactions affect student achievement. Long-term teacher-student relationships result in improved student performance (Burke, 1996). Higher student grades result when teachers and students have congruent values (Battle, 1954). Teacher-student interaction has a positive influence on eighth grade achievement when considering culture (Smith-Maddox, 1998). Black student achievement has a high correlation with warm and supportive teachers (St. John, 1971).

Minority students have beliefs regarding student achievement and teacher-student relationships. According to Slaughter-Defoe and Carlson (1990), Black students believe their academic achievement increases when they have positive relationships with teachers. Black students also believe that increases in positive feelings affect academic achievement when teachers become responsive to the students' personal lives. Conversely, Black students believe that their poor academic performance results from teachers who lack concern for them and engage in negative gossip regarding students (Mirón & Lauria, 1998). Black and Latino urban high school students believe their underachievement results when teachers lack caring interpersonal skills to develop positive teacher-student relationships (Lee, 1999).

The interpersonal relationship between students and teachers has a profound impact on instructional activities and outcomes (Powell & Caseau, 2004). Teachers respond to their favorite students by creating a warmer and more positive classroom atmosphere, providing superior feedback on how they are performing, teach challenging material, and increase opportunities to respond to questions (Rosenthal, 1974). Teacher warmth increases student vocabulary and arithmetic achievement (Christiansen, 1960). Warm relationships between teachers and students motivate students to meet teachers' requests for compliance (Bidwell, 1965). Expressing warmth toward minority students without accompanying the friendliness with challenging academic standards is just as debilitating to students as expressing overt hostility (Dornbusch et al., 1975). Student noncompliance with teacher requests can produce a negative teacher-student classroom relationship. According to Bates (1976):

> A different possibility for how a negative adult-child feedback loop might produce unfortunate outcomes for a child is that the teacher's negativity might raise the child's chronic level of anxiety in the classroom that might inhibit learning of new material and not just performance of previously learned skills. (p. 1087)

Students are more willing to develop positive relationships with teachers who tend to get emotionally involved with their teaching (Grossack, 1955).

Students have indicated certain positive beliefs regarding teachers that can influence instruction and classroom relationship development. High school students believe good teachers express enthusiastic energy that translates into excitement and good teachers are nice but not rude (Whitney, Leonard, Leonard, Camelio, & Camelio, 2005). Sixth grade students believe the best teachers are flexible and fair when they respect children by their willingness to listen to students (Shedlin, 1986). Sixth grade students believe teachers make learning useful when they use cross-curricular teaching. Sixth grade students believe the best teachers have demanding expectations, are enthusiastic and resourceful, and help students with their work. Elementary school students believe good teachers (a) make lessons fun, (b) ask easy questions, (c) give breaks during lesson time, (d) do not give difficult homework, (e) treat all students well, (f) treat all students equally, (g) are willing to listen to students, (h) act like parents to students, (i) are interested in each student individually, (j) share students' problems, concerns, and joys, and (k) love students (Aksoy, 1998). It is important that students feel comfortable and at ease in the classroom (Ashmore & Project M.E.D.I.A, 1984). Children who have positive feelings regarding teachers have favorable classroom behavior (Davidson & Lang, 1960).

# REFERENCES

Abrahams, R., & Gay, G. (1972). Talking Back in the Classroom. In R. Abrahams (Ed.), *Language and Cultural Diversity in American Education* (pp. 200-207). Englewood Cliffs, NJ: Prentice Hall.

Aiello, J., & Jones, S. (1971). Field study of the proxemic behavior of young school children in three subcultural groups. *Journal of Personality and Social Psychology, 19(3)*, 351-356.

Aksoy, N. (1998). Opinions of Upper Elementary Students About a "Good Teacher" Case Study in turkey. *ED428042.*

Allport, G. (1954). *The Nature of Prejudice.* Cambridge, MA: Addison-Wesley.

Amos, R. (1952). The Accuracy of Negro and White Children's Predictions of Teachers' Attitudes Toward of Negro Students. *Journal of Negro Education, 21(2)*, 125-135.

Anderson, J., Anderson, P., Murphy, M., & Wendt-Wasco, N. (1986). Teachers' Reports of Students' Nonverbal Communication in the Classroom: A Developmental Study in Grades K - 12. *Communication Education, 34(4)*, 292-307.

Anderson, J., Norton, R., & Nussbaum, J. (1981). Three Investigations Exploring Relationships Between Perceived Teacher Communication Behaviors and Student Learning. *Communication Education, 30(4)*, 377-392.

Asante, M., & Davis, A. (1985). Black and White Communication: Analyzing Work Place Encounters. *Journal of Black Studies, 16*(1), 77-93.

Ashmore, J., & Project M.E.D.I.A. (1984). *A Manual of Instructional Strategies.* Unpublished manuscript, Department of Instructional and Support Services Jefferson County Public Schools.

Baron, R., Tom, D., & Cooper, H. (1985). Social class, race, and teacher expectations. In J. Dusek, V. Hall

& W. Meyer (Eds.), *Teacher Expectancies.* Hillsdale, NJ: Lawrence Erlbaum.

Bates, J. (1976). Effects of Children's Nonverbal Behavior Upon Adults. *Child Development, 47(4)*, 1079-1088.

Battle, H. (1954). Social-class variations in the teacher-pupil relationship. *Journal of Educational Sociology, 25*, 451-465.

Bauer, E. (1973). Personal space: A Study of Blacks and Whites. *Sociometry, 36(3)*, 402-408.

Baxter, J. (1970). Interpersonal Spacing in Natural Settings. *Sociometry, 33(4)*, 444-456.

Bennett, C. (1997). Teaching students as they would be taught: The importance of cultural perspective. In B. Shade (Ed.), *Culture, Style, and the Educative Process: Making Schools Work for Racially Diverse Students* (2nd, pp. 129-142). Springfield, Ill.: Charles C. Thomas.

Bidwell, C. (1965). The school as a formal organization. In J. March (Ed.), *Handbook of organizations.* Chicago: Rand McNally.

Birdwhistell, R. (1970). *Kinetics and Context; essays on body motion communication.* Philadelphia: University of Pennsylvania Press.

Blanck, P., & Rosenthal, R. (1982). Developing strategies for decoding "leaky" messages: On learning how and when to decode discrepant and consistent social communications. In R. Feldman (Ed.), *Development of nonverbal behavior in children.* New York: Springer-Verlag.

Borkowski, J., & Krause, A. (1983). Racial differences in intelligence: This importance of the executive system. *Intelligence, 7(4)*, 379-395.

Bourdieu, P., & Passeron, J. (1979). *The Inheritors: French Students and Their Relation to Culture.* Chicago: University of Chicago Press.

Boykin, W. (1986). The Triple Quandary and the Schooling of Afro-American Children. In U. Neisser (Ed.), *The School Achievement of Minority Children* (pp. 57-92). Hillsdale, NJ: Lawrence Erlbaum.

Braum, C. (1976). Teacher Expectations: Socio psychological Dynamics. *Review of Educational Research, 46(2)*, 185-213.

Brophy, J. (1981). Teacher Praise: A Functional Analysis. *Review of Educational Research, 51*(1), 5-32.

Brophy, J. (1983). Research on the Self-Fulfilling Prophecy and Teacher Expectations. *Journal of Educational Psychology, 75(5)*, 631-661.

Brophy, J., & Evertson, C. (1976). *Learning from teaching: a developmental perspective.* Boston: Allyn.

Brophy, J., & Good, T. (1970). Teacher's Communication of Differential Expectations for Children's Classroom Performance: Some Behavioral Data. *Journal of Educational Psychology, 61(5)*, 365-374.

Brophy, J., & Good, T. (1974). *Teacher-student relationships.* New York: Holt, Rinehart, & Winston.

Brophy, J., Evertson, C., Anderson, L., Baum, M., & Crawford, J. (1976). Student Attribute Study: A Preliminary Report. *ED121799.*

Brown, D. (1999). Proven Strategies for Improving Learning & Achievement. *ED430179.*

Brown, D. (2003). Urban Teachers' Use of Culturally Responsive Managements Strategies. *Theory into Practice, 42*(4), 277-282.

Brown, W., Payne, L., Lankewich, C., & Cornell, L. (1970). Praise, Criticism, and Race. *Elementary School Journal, 70(7)*, 373-377.

Bryant, J., & Zillman, D. (1988). Using Humor to Promote Learning in the Classroom. *Journal of Children in Contemporary Society, 20*(1-2), 49-78.

Buriel, R. (1983). Teacher-student interactions and their relationship to student achievement: A comparison of Mexican-American children and Anglo-American Children. *Journal of Educational Psychology, 75(6)*, 889-897.

Burke, D. (1996). Multi-year teacher/student relationships are a long-overdue arrangement. *Phi Delta Kappan, 77*(5), 360-361.

Burmal, J. (1970). *Mexican-Americans in the United States: A Reader.* New York: Harper & Row.

Byalick, R., & Bershoff, D. (1974). Reinforcement practices of black and white teachers in integrated classrooms. *Journal of Educational Psychology, 66*(4), 473-480.

Byers, P., & Byers, H. (1972). Nonverbal communication and the education of children. In C. Cazden, V. John & D. Hymes (Eds.), *Functions of Language in the Classroom.* New York: Academic Press.

Chaikin, A., Gillen, B., Derlega, V., Heinen, J., & Wilson, M. (1978). Students' reactions to teachers' physical attractiveness and nonverbal behavior. *Psychology in the Schools, 15(3)*, 588-595.

Chappell, C., & McCoy, L. (2003). Studies in Teaching. In Wake Forest University (Ed.), *Research Digest: Research Projects Presented at Annual Research Forum.* Winston-Salem, NC: Wake Forest University.

Chenfeld, M. (1990). My loose is tooth! Kidding around with the kids. *Young Children, 46*(1), 56-60.

Christiansen, C. (1960). Relationships between pupil achievement, pupil affect-need, teacher warmth, and teacher permissiveness. *Journal of Educational Psychology, 51(3)*, 169-174.

Clark, K. (1955). *Prejudice and your child.* Boston: Beacon Press.

Clegg, A., & Megson, B. (1968). *Children in distress.* Harmondsworth, Middx: Penguin.

Clifton, R. (1981). The Effects of Students' Ethnicity and Sex on the Expectations of Teachers. *Interchange, 12(1)*, 31-38.

Coates, B. (1972). White Adult Behavior Toward Black and White Children. *Child Development, 43(1)*, 143-154.

Cohen, R. (1969). Conceptual Styles, Culture Conflict, and Nonverbal Tests of Intelligence. *American Anthropologist, 71(5)*, 828-856.

Colier, M. (1988). A Comparison of conversations among and between domestic culture and groups: How intra-and intercultural communication competencies vary. *Communication Quarterly, 36(2)*, 122-144.

Collier, J., & Powell, R. (1990). Ethnicity, Instructional Communication and Classroom Systems. *Communication Quarterly, 38*(4), 334-349.

Colwell, C., & Wigle, S. (1984). Applicability of Humor in the Reading/Language Arts Curriculum. *Reading World, 24*(2), 73-80.

Comer, J. (1976). The oppositional child: Is the black child at greater risk? In E. Anthony & D. Gilpin (Eds.), *Three clinical faces of childhood.* New York: Spectrum.

Cooper, H. (1979). Pygmalion Grows up: A Model for Teacher Expectation Communication and Performance Influence. *Review of Educational Research, 49(3)*, 389-410.

Cooper, H., Baron, R., & Lowe, C. (1997). The importance of race and social class information of expectations about academic performance. *Journal of Educational Psychology, 67(2)*, 312-319.

Cooper, P., & Simmonds, C. (1999). *Communication for the Classroom Teacher* (6th). Boston: Allyn & Bacon.

Cordeiro, P., & Carspecken, P. (1993). How a minority of the minority succeed: A case study of twenty Hispanic achievers. *Qualitative Studies in Education, 6*(4), 277-290.

Corsini, V., & Fogliasso, C. (1997). A Descriptive Study of the Use of the Black Communication Style by African Americans within an Organization. *Journal of Technical Writing and Communication, 27*(1), 33-47.

Cummins, J. (1986). Empowering Minority Students: A Framework for Intervention. *Harvard Educational Review, 56(1)*, 18-36.

Cureton, G. (1978). Using a black learning style. *The Reading Teacher, 1(7)*, 751-756.

Dace, K. (1994). Dissonance in European-American and Africa-American Communication. *The Western Journal of Black Studies, 18*(1), 18-26.

Damico, S. (1983). Two Worlds of School: Differences in the Photographs of Black and White Adolescents. *ED230662.*

Datta, L., Schaefer, E., & Davis, M. (1968). Sex and Scholastic Aptitude as Variables in Teachers' Ratings of the Adjustment and Classroom Behavior of Negro and Other Seventh-grade Students. *Journal of Educational Psychology, 59(2)*, 94-101.

Davidson, H., & Lang, G. (1960). Children's perceptions of their teachers' feelings toward them related to self-perception, school achievement, and behavior. *Journal of Experimental Education, 29(2)*, 107-118.

Delgado-Gaitan, C. (1992). School Matters in the Mexican-American Home: Socializing Children to Education. *American Educational Research Journal, 29*(3), 495-513.

Delgado-Gaitan, C. (1994). Consejos: The Power of Cultural Narratives. *Anthropology and Education Quarterly, 25(3)*, 298-316.

Dew, A., & Ward, C. (1993). The Effects of Ethnicity and Culturally Congruent and Incongruent Nonverbal Behaviors on Interpersonal Attraction. *Journal of Applied Social Psychology, 23(17)*, 1376-1389.

DiStefano, J. (1970). *Interpersonal Perceptions of Field Independent and Dependent Teachers and Students.*

London: University of Western Ontario Working Paper Series 43.

Dornbusch, S., Massey, G., & Scott, M. (1975). *Racism Without Racists: Institutional Racism in Urban Schools.* Stanford: Stanford University Publications.

Dreeben, R. (1968). *On What is Learned in School.* Reading, MA: Addison Wesley Publishing.

Duncan, B. (1978). The Development of Spatial Behavior Norms in Black and White Primary School Children. *Journal of Black Psychology, 5(1)*, 33-41.

Dusek, J. (1975). Do Teachers Bias Children's Learning? *Review of Educational Research, 45(4)*, 661-684.

Eaves, R. (1975). Teacher race, student race, and the behavior problem checklist. *Journal of Abnormal Child Psychology, 3*(1), 1-9.

Entwise, D., & Webster, M. (1974). Expectations in Mixed Racial Groups. *Sociology of Education, 47*, 301-318.

Erickson, F. (1979). Talking down: Some cultural sources of miscommunication in interracial interviews. In A. Wolfgang (Ed.), *Nonverbal behavior: Applications and cultural implications* (pp. 99-126). New York: Academic Press.

Erickson, F. (1987). Transformation and School Success: The Politics and Culture of Educational Achievement. *Anthropology and Education Quarterly, 18*(4), 335-356.

Erickson, F. (1997). Culture in society and in educational practices. In J. Banks & C. Banks (Eds.), *Multicultural education: issues and perspectives* (3$^{rd}$, pp. 32-60). Needham Heights, MA: Allyn & Bacon.

Evertson, C., Anderson, C., Anderson, L., & Brophy, J. (1980). Relationships Between Classroom Behaviors and Student Outcomes in Junior High Mathematics and English Classes. *American Educational Research Journal, 17(1)*, 43-60.

Farkas, G., Grobe, R., & Shaun, Y. (1990). Cultural Resources and School Success: Gender, ethnicity, and poverty groups within an urban school district. *American Sociological Review, 55(1)*, 127-142.

Feldman, R. (1985). Nonverbal Behavior, Race, and the Classroom Teacher. *Theory into Practice, 24*(1), 45-49.

Feldman, R., & Donohue, L. (1978). Nonverbal Communication of Affect in Interracial Dyads. *Journal of Educational Psychology, 70(6)*, 979-987.

Fordham, S., & Ogbu, J. (1986). Black students' school success: Coping with the burden of "acting white". *Urban Review, 18*, 176-206.

Garcia, R. (1984). Countering Classroom Discrimination. *Theory into Practice, 23*(2), 104-109.

Garcia, S., & Guerra, P. (2003). Do We Truly Believe All Children Can Learn? Implications for Comprehensive School Reform. *Adelante Newsletter, 4*(1), 5.

Gates, D. (1998). Diversity Issues in Teaching: Cultural Sensitivity in the Classroom. *ED425482.*

Gay, G. (1975). Cultural Differences Important in Education of Black Children. *Momentum,* 30-31.

Gay, G. (1975). Teachers' achievement expectations of and classroom interactions with ethnically different students. *Contemporary Education, 46(3)*, 166-172.

Gay, G. (2000). *Culturally Responsive Teaching: Theory, Research, and Practice.* New York: Teachers College Press 2000.

Gay, G., & Abrahams, R. (1972). Black culture in the classroom. In R. Abrahams & R. Troike (Eds.), *Language and Cultural Diversity in American Education* (pp. 67-84). Englewood Cliffs: Prentice-Hall.

Gilbert, S., & Gay, G. (1985). Improving the Success in School of Poor Black Children. *Phi Delta Kappan, 67*(2), 133-137.

Glasser, W. (1990). *The Quality School: Managing students without coercion* (1st). New York: Harper and Row.

Good, T., & Brophy, J. (1972). Behavioral expression of teacher attitudes. *Journal of Educational Psychology, 63(6)*, 617-624.

Good, T., & Grouws, D. (1977). Teaching Effects: A Process-Product Study in Fourth Grade Mathematics Classrooms. *Journal of Teacher Education, 28(3)*, 49-54.

Goodenow, C. (1993). Classroom Belonging Among Early Adolescent Students: Relationships to Motivation and Achievement. *Journal of Early Adolescence, 13(1)*, 21-43.

Goor, M. (1989). Humor in the classroom: Options for Enhancing Learning. *ED332090.*

Gordon, E., Miller, F., & Rollock, D. (1990). Coping with Communicentric Bias in Knowledge Production in the Social Sciences. *Educational Researcher, 19(3)*, 14-19.

Gordon, G. (1999). Teacher Talent and Urban Schools. *Phi Delta Kappan, 81*(4), 304-307.

Gorham, J. (1987). *Sixth grade Students' Perceptions of Good Teachers* (ED359164).

Gorham, J. (1988). The Relationship Between Verbal Teacher Immediacy Behaviors and Student Learning. *Communication Education, 37(1)*, 40-53.

Grossack, M. (1955). Effects of Variations in Teacher Role Behavior on the Student-Teacher Relationship. *The Journal of Educational Psychology, 46*(7), 433-436.

Grossman, H. (1995). *Educating Hispanic Students: Implications for instruction, classroom management, counseling, and assessment* (2nd). Springfield, Ill.: Charles C. Thomas.

Grossman, H. (1998). *Ending Discrimination in Special Education.* Springfield, Ill.: Charles C. Thomas.

Guardo, C. (1969). Personal Space in Children. *Child Development, 40(1)*, 141-151.

Guardo, C., & Meisels, M. (1971). Factor Structure of Children's Personal Space Schemata. *Child Development, 42(4)*, 1307-1312.

Hale, J. (1982). *Black children: Their roots, culture, and learning styles.* Provo, Utah: Bringham Young University.

Hall, V., & Kaye, D. (1977). Patterns of early cognitive development among boys in four subcultural groups. *Journal of Educational Psychology, 69(1)*, 66-87.

Hall, E. (1966). *The Hidden Dimension* (1st). New York: Doubleday.

Hall, E. (1989). Unstated features of the cultural context of learning. *The Educational Forum, 54(1)*, 21-34.

Halpern, F. (1973). *Survival black/white.* New York: Pergamon Press.

Hanna, J. (1988). *Disruptive school behavior: Class, race, and culture.* New York: Holmes & Meier.

Heal, K. (1978). Misbehavior Among School Children: The role of the school in strategies for prevention. *Policy and Politics, 6*, 321-332.

Heath, S. (1983). *Ways with Words: Language, Life, and Work in Communities and Classrooms.* New York: Cambridge University.

Heller, D. (1996). Another Look at Student Motivation. *ED398524.*

Heller, D., & Scottile, J. (1996). Another Look at Student Motivation: A qualitative study. *ED398524.*

Hidalgo, N. (1994). Profile of a Puerto Rican Family's Support for School Achievement. *Equity and Choice, 10*(2), 14-22.

Hill, P., Lake, R., Celio, M., Campbell, C., Herdman, P., & Bulkey, K. (2001). A Study of Charter School Accountability. Washington, DC: US Department of Education.

Hillard, A. (1989). Teachers and cultural styles in a pluralistic society. *NEA Today, 7(6)*, 65-69.

Hillman, S., & Davenport, G. (1978). Teacher-student interactions in desegregated schools. *Journal of Educational Psychology, 70(4)*, 545-553.

Hirschberg, N., Jones, L., & Haggerty, E. (1978). What's in a face: Individual difference in face perception. *Journal of Research in Personality, 12*, 488-499.

Howard, T. (2001). Telling their side of the story: African-American students' perceptions of culturally relevant teaching. *The Urban Review, 33*(2), 131-149.

Hoy, W. (1968). The influence of experience on the beginning teachers. *The School Review, 76(3)*, 312-323.

Hughes, D. (1973). An Experimental Investigation of the Effects of Pupil Responding and Teacher Reacting on Pupil Achievement. *American Educational Research Journal, 10(1)*, 21-37.

Hurlock, E. (1924). The Value of Praise and Reproof as Incentives for Children. *Archeology Psychology, 71,* 1-78.

Ikeda, T., & Beebe, S. (1992). A Review of Teacher Nonverbal Immediacy: Implications for Intercultural Research. *ED349592.*

Irvine, J. (1990). *Black Students and school failure: Policies, practices, and prescriptions.* New York: Greenwood Press.

Jenkins, C., & Bainer, D. (1991). Common Instructional Problems in the Multicultual Classroom. *ED330279.*

Jensen, A. (1969). How much can we boost IQ and scholastic achievement? *Harvard Education Review, 39(41),* 1-123.

Johnson, D. (1971). Black Kinesics: Some Non-Verbal Communication Patterns in Black Culture. *EJ52204.*

Joint Center for Economic and Policy Studies,
Committee on Policy and Racial Justice. (1989).
*Visions of a better way: A black appraisal of public schooling.* Washington, DC: Author.

Jones, S., & Aiello, J. (1973). Proxemic behavior of black and white first, third, and fifth grade children. *Journal of Personality and Social Psychology, 25(1)*, 21-27.

Kearney, P. (1984). Perceptual discrepancies in teacher communication style. *Communication Education, 13*, 95-108.

Keith, T., Tornatzky, L., & Pettigrew, L. (1974). An Analysis of Verbal and Nonverbal Classroom Teaching Behaviors. *The Journal of Experimental Education, 42*(4), 30-38.

Knapp, M. (1971). The role of nonverbal communication in the classroom. *Theory into Practice, 10(4)*, 243-249.

Knight, S., & Waxman, H. (1991). Students cognition and classroom instruction. In H. Waxman & H. Walberg (Eds.), *Effective teaching: Current research.* Berkeley, CA: McCutchan.

Koch, R. (1971). The Teacher and Nonverbal Communication. *Theory into Practice, 10(4)*, 231-242.

Koch, R. (1971). Nonverbal Observables. *Theory into Practice, 10*(4), 288-294.

Kochman, T. (1981). *Black and White styles in conflict.* Chicago: University Chicago Press.

Kohn, A. (1996). *Beyond discipline: From compliance to community.* Alexandria, VA: Association for Supervision and Curriculum Development.

Kryston, V., Smith, M., Collins, S, Hamilton, M. (1986). Facets: The place of humor and sarcasm in the English class. *The English Journal, 75(4)*, 18-21.

Kuykendall, C. (1992). *From rage to hope: Strategies for reflecting Black and Hispanic students.* Bloomington, in: National Educational Service.

Laosa, L. (1980). Maternal Teaching Strategies in Chicano and Anglo-American Families: The influence of culture and education on maternal behaviors. *Child Development, 51(3)*, 759-765.

Leacock, E. (1969). *Teacing and Learning in City Schools.* New York: Basic Books.

Leathers, D. (1997). *Successful Nonverbal Communication: Principles and Applications ($3^{rd}$).* Boston: Allyn and Bacon.

Lee, P. (1999). In Their Own Voices: An Ethnographic Study of Low-Achieving Student within the Content of School Reform. *Urban Education, 34*(2), 214-244.

Leiding, D. (2006). *Racial Bias in the Classroom: Can teachers reach all children?* Lanham, MD: Rowman & Littlefield Education.

Lerner, R., Karabeneck, S., & Meisels, M. (1975). Effect of age and sex on the development of personal space schemata towards body build. *Journal of Genetic Psychology, 127*, 91-101.

Liebman, M. (1970). The effects of sex and race norms on personal space. *Environment and Behavior, 2(2)*, 208-246.

Locke, D. (1992). *Increasing multi-cultural understanding: A comprehensive model.* Newbury Park, CA: Sage Publications.

Lucas, T., Henze, R., & Donato, R. (1990). Promoting the Success of Latino Language-Minority Students: An exploratory study of six high schools. *Harvard Educational Review, 60(3)*, 315-340.

Marchesani, L., & Adams, M. (1992). Dynamics of diversity in the teaching-learning process: A faculty development model of analysis and action. *New Direction for Teaching and Learning, 52*, 9-20.

McCarty, J. (Trans.). (1981). In T. Kochman (Ed.), *Black and White Styles in Conflict.* Chicago: The University of Chicago Press.

McClure, E. (1978). Teacher and pupil questions and responses and the Mexican-American child. *The Bilingual Review: La Rivista Bilingüe, 5,* 40-44.

McDermott, R. (1977). Social relations as contexts for learning in school. *Harvard Educational Review, 47(2),* 198-213.

McDonald, F., & Elias, P. (1976). *The effects of teacher performance on pupil learning. Beginning Teacher Evaluation Study, Phase I, Final Report vol.1.* Princeton, NJ: Educational Testing Service.

Mehrabian, A. (1968). Communication without words. *Psychology Today, 2,* 51-52.

Meisels, M., & Guardo, C. (1969). Development of Personal Space Schemata. *Child Development, 40(4),* 1167-1178.

Meyer, J. (2000). Humor as a double-edged sword: Four functions of humor in communication. *Communication Theory, 10(3)*, 310-331.

Milburn, T. (2000). Inferring Cultural Learning Styles - Puerto Ricans in the US. *ED448492.*

Millard, R., & Stimpson, D. (1980). Enjoyment and productivity as a function of classroom seating location. *Perceptual and Motor Skills, 50*, 429-444.

Mirón, L., & Lauria, M. (1998). Student Voice as Agency: Resistance and Accommodation in Inner-City Schools. *Anthropology and Education Quarterly, 29(2)*, 189-213.

Moll, L. (1988). Some key issues in teaching Latino students. *Language Arts, 65*(5), 465-472.

Morales-Jones, C. (1998). Understanding Hispanic Culture: From Tolerance to Acceptance. *The Delta Gamma Bulletin, 64*(4), 13-17.

Morgan, H. (1981). Factors concerning cognitive development and learning differentiation among

Black children. In A. Harrison (Ed.), *Conference on Empirical Research in Black Psychology.* Rochester, MI: Oakland University.

Morganett, L. (1991). Good teacher-student relationships: A key element for classroom motivation and management. *Education, 112(2)*, 260-264.

Morris, M. (1981). *Saying and meaning in Puerto Rico: Some problems in the ethnography of discourse* (1st). Oxford, New York: Pergamon Press.

Murray, C., & Malmgren, K. (2005). Implementing a teacher-student relationship program in a high-poverty urban school: Effects on social, emotional, and academic adjustment and lessons learned. *Journal of School Psychology, 43(2)*, 137-152.

Norton, B. (1995). *The Quality Classroom Manager.* Amityville, NY: Baywood.

Nussbaum, J. (1992). Effective Teacher Behaviors. *Communication Education, 41(2)*, 167-180.

Obidah, J., & Manheim Teel, K. (2001). *Because of the kids: Facing racial and cultural differences in schools.* New York: Teachers College Press.

Ogbu, J. (1974). *The Next Generation: An Ethnography of Education in an Urban Neighborhood.* New York: Academic Press.

Ogbu, J. (1978). *Minority education and caste: The American system in cross-cultural perspective.* New York: Academic Press.

Ogbu, J. (1982). Cultural Discontinuities and Schooling. *Anthropology and Education Quarterly, 13*(4), 290-307.

Ogbu, J. (1983). Minority Status and Schooling in Plural Societies. *Comparative Education Review, 27*(2), 168-190.

Ogbu, J. (1987). Variability in Minority School Performance: A Problem in Search of an Explanation. *Anthropology and Education Quarterly, 18(4)*, 312-334.

Ogbu, J. (1988). Cultural diversity and human development. In D. Slaughter (Ed.), *New Directions in Child Development: Vol. 42. black children and poverty: A developmental perspective* (pp. 11-28). San Francisco: Jossey-Bass.

Ogbu, J. (1992). Adaptation to Minority Status and Impact on School Success. *Theory Into Practice, 31*(4), 287-295.

Ogbu, J. (1992). Understanding Cultural Diversity and Learning. *Educational Researcher, 21*(8), 5-14 + 24.

O'Leary, K., & O'Leary, S. (1977). *Classroom management: The successful use of behavior modification* (2nd). New York: Pergamon.

Orasanu, J., Lee, C., & Scribner, S. (1979). The Development of Category Organization and Free Recall: Ethnic and economic group comparisons. *Child Development, 50(4)*, 1100-1109.

Orbe, M. (1994). "Remember, it's always whites' ball": Descriptions of African American male communication. *Communication Quarterly, 42(3)*, 287-300.

Ornstein, A., & Levine, D. (1990). Class, Race, and Achievement. *Education Digest, 55(9)*, 11-14.

Ortiz, F. (1988). Hispanic-American children's experiences in classrooms: A comparison between Hispanic and non-Hispanic children. In L. Weis (Ed.), *Class, race, and gender in American education* (pp. 63-86). New York: State University of New York Press.

Parker, L., & French, R. (1971). A Description of student behavior: Verbal and nonverbal. *Theory into Practice, 10(4)*, 276-281.

Pasteur, A., & Toldson, I. (1982). *Roots of soul: The psychology of Black expressiveness: An unprecedented and intensive examination of Black*

*Folk Expressions in the Enrichment of Life.*
Garden City, NJ: Anchor Press/Doubleday Press.

Patchen, M. (1982). *Black-White contact in schools: Its social and academic effects.* West Lafayette, IN.: Perdue University Press.

Patthey-Chavez, G. (1993). High School as an Arena for Cultural Conflict and Association for Latino Angelinos. *Anthropology & Educational Quarterly, 24(1)*, 33-60.

Patton, D., Warring, D., Frank, K., & Hunter, S. (1993). Multicultural Message: Nonverbal Communication in the Classroom. *ED362519.*

Pianta, R. (1999). *Enhancing relationships between children and teachers* (1st). Washington, DC: American Psychological Association.

Plax, T., Kearney, P., McCroskey, J., & Richmond, V. (1986). Power in the Classroom VI: Verbal Control Strategies, Nonverbal Immediacy and Affective Learning. *Communication Education, 35(1)*, 43-55.

Pollack, J., & Freda, P. (1997). Humor, learning, and socialization in middle level classrooms. *The Clearing House, 70(4)*, 176-179.

Pollard, D. (1989). Against the Odds: A Profile of Underclass Achievers. *Journal of Negro Education, 58(3)*, 297-308.

Pomery, E. (1999). The teacher-student relationship in secondary school: Insights from excluded students. *British Journal, 20*(4), 465-82.

Powell, R., & Caseau, D. (2004). *Classroom Communication and Diversity: Enhancing Instructional Practice.* Mahwah, New Jersey: Lawrence Erlbaum Associates.

Quiroz, P. (2001). The Silencing of Latino Student "Voice": Puerto Rican and Mexican Narratives in Eighth Grade and High School. *Anthropology & Education Quarterly, 32*(3), 326-349.

Ramerez, M., & Price-Williams, D. (1974). Cognitive styles of children of three ethnic groups in the

United States. *Journal of Cross-Cultural Psychology, 5*, 212-219.

Rareshide, S. (1993). Implications for Teachers' Use of Humor in the Classroom. *ED359165.*

Resnick, M., Bearman, P., Blum, R., Bauman, K., Harris, K., & Jones, R. (1997). Protecting adolescents from harm: Findings from the national longitudinal study on adolescent health. *Journal of the American Medical Association, 278*, 823-832.

Richmond, V. (2002). Teacher nonverbal immediacy: Use and outcomes. In J. Chesebro & J. McCroskely (Eds.), *Communication for Teachers* (pp. 65-82). Boston: Allyn & Bacon.

Rosenfield, L., & Richman, J. (1999). Supportive Communication and School Outcomes: Part II. Academically "at-risk" Low Income High School Students. *Communication Education, 48(4)*, 294-307.

Rosenshine, R. (1976). Recent Research on Teacher Behaviors and Student Achievement. *Journal of Teacher Education, 27(1)*, 61-64.

Rosenthal, B. (1974). *On the psychology of the self-fulfilling prophecy: Further evidence for Pygmalion effects and mediating mechanisms* (Vol. 53, pp. 1-28). New York: MSS Modular Publications, Inc.

Rosenthal, R., & Jacobson, L. (1968). *Pygmalion in the classroom: Teacher expectation and pupils'' intellectual development.* New York: Holt, Rinehart, & Winston.

Rothbart, M., Dalfen, S., & Barrett, R. (1971). Effects of Teacher's Expectancy on Student-Teacher Interaction. *Journal of Educational Psychology, 62*(1), 49-54.

Rubio, O. (1995). "Yo Soy Voluntaria": Volunteering in a Dual-Language School. *Urban Education, 29*(4), 396-409.

Rubovits, P., & Maehr, M. (1973). Pygmalion black and white. *Journal of Personality and Social Psychology, 25(2)*, 210-218.

Rutter, M., Maughan, B., Mortimore, P., Ouston, J., & Smith, A. (1979). *Fifteen Thousand Hours: Secondary schools and their effects in children.* Cambridge, Mass.: Harvard University Press.

Rychlak, J. (1975). Affective assessment, intelligence, social class, and racial learning style. *Journal of Personality and Social Psychology, 32(6)*, 989-995.

Rychlak, J., Hewitt, C., & Hewitt, J. (1973). Affective evaluation, word quality, and verbal learning styles of black versus white junior college females. *Journal of Personality and Social Psychology, 27(2)*, 248-255.

Safilios-Rothchild, C. (1979). *Sex-role socialization and sex discrimination: A synthesis and critique of the literature.* Washington, DC: National Institute of Education.

Saracho, N., & Dayton, C. (1980). Relationships of Teachers' Cognitive Styles to Pupils' Academic Achievement Gains. *Journal of Educational Psychology, 72(4)*, 544-549.

Sava, F. (2002). Causes and effects of teacher conflict-inducing attitudes towards pupils: a path analysis model. *Teaching and Teacher Education, 18(8)*, 1007-1021.

Schusler, R. (1971). Nonverbal Communication in the Elementary Classroom. *Theory into Practice, 10*(4), 282-287.

Schwebel, A., & Cherlin, D. (1972). Physical and social distancing in teacher-pupil relationships. *Journal of Educational Psychology, 63(6)*, 543-550.

Sedlacek, W., & Brooks Jr., G. (1976). *Racism in American Education: A model for change.* Chicago: Nelson-Hall.

Shade, B. (1978). Social-Psychological Characteristics of Achieving Black Children. *The Negro Educational Review, 29*(2), 80-85.

Shade, B. (1981). Racial variation in perceptual differentiation. *Perceptual and Motor Skills, 52*, 243-248.

Shade, B. (1982). Afro-American Cognitive Style: A Variable in School Success? *Review of Educational Research, 52*(2), 219-244.

Shade, B. (1983). *Afro-American Patterns of Cognition.* Madison: University of Wisconsin Center for Education Research.

Shade, B. (1989). The influence of perceptual development on cognitive style: Cross-Ethnic Comparisons. *Early Child Development and Care, 51*, 137-155.

Shade, B. (1994). Understanding the African Learner. In E. Hollins, J. King & W. Haemin (Eds.), *Teaching Diverse Populations: Formulating a Knowledge Base.* Albany: State University of New York Press.

Shade, B. (1997). The Culture and Style of Mexican-American Society. In B. Shade (Ed.), *Culture, Style, and the Educative Process: Making Schools Work for Racially Diverse Students.* Springfield, Ill: Charles C. Thomas.

Shade, B. (1997). African-American Cognitive Patterns: A review of the Research. In B. Shade (Ed.), *Culture, Style, and the Educative Process: Making Schools Work for Racially Diverse Students.* Springfield, Ill.: Charles C. Thomas.

Shade, B. (1997). Culture and Learning Style within the African-American Community. In B. Shade (Ed.), *Culture, Style, and the Educative Process: Making Schools Work for Racially Diverse Students.* Springfield, Ill.: Charles C. Thomas.

Shade, B. (1997). Culture: The Key to Adaptation. In B. Shade (Ed.), *Culture, Style and the Educative Process: Making Schools Work for Racially Diverse Students.* Springfield, Ill.: Charles C. Thomas.

Shade, B. (1997). Teaching to an African-American Cognitive Style. In B. Shade (Ed.), *Culture, Style and the Educative Process: Making schools work for racially diverse students.* Springfield, ILL.: Charles C. Thomas.

Shade, B., Kelly, C., & Oberg, M. (1997). *Creating Culturally Responsive Classroom* (1$^{st}$). Washington, DC: American Psychological Association.

Shanoski, L., & Hranitz, J. (1991). A Foundation for Excellence in Teaching. *ED356212.*

Shedlin, A. (1986). 487 sixth graders can't be wrong. *Principal, 66(1)*, 53.

Shibles, W. (1978). Humor: A critical analysis for young people. *ED171643.*

Shirley, A. (2003). Wrong Answers and Raised Hands: The Relationship between Teacher Responses to Wrong Answers and Class Participation. In L. McCoy (Ed.), *Studies in Teaching: 2003 Research Digest* (pp. 121-125). Winston-Salem, NC: Wake Forest University.

Shuter, R. (1976). Nonverbal Communication: Proxemics and Tactility in Latin America. *Journal of Communication, 26*(3), 46-52.

Sigel, I., Anderson, L., & Shapiro, H. (1966). Categorization behavior of lower-and middle-class Negro preschool children: Difference in Dealing with Representation of Familiar Objects. *Journal of Negro Education, 35(3)*, 218-229.

Silberman, M. (1969). Behavioral expression of teacher's attitudes toward elementary school students. *Journal of Educational Psychology, 60(5)*, 402-407.

Simmons, W. (1979). *The Role of Cultural Salience in Ethnic and Social Class Difference in Cognitive Performance.* Unpublished doctoral dissertation, Cornell University.

Simpson, A., & Erickson, M. (1983). Teachers' Verbal and Nonverbal Communication Patterns as a Function of Teacher Race, Student Gender, and Student Race. *American Educational Research Journal, 20(2)*, 183-198.

Skinner, E., & Belmount, M. (1993). Motivation in the classroom: Reciprocal effects of teacher behavior and student engagement across the school year. *Journal of Educational Psychology, 85(4)*, 571-581.

Slaughter-Defoe, D., & Carlson, K. (1996). Young African American and Latino children in High-Poverty Urban Schools: How They Perceive School Climate. *Journal of Negro Education, 65*(1), 60-70.

Slavin, R. (1983). *Cooperative Learning.* New York: Longman Press.

Smith, W., & Drumming, S. (1989). On the strategies blacks employ in deductive reasoning. *Journal of Black Psychology, 16*, 1-22.

Smith-Maddox, R. (1998). Defining Culture as a Dimension of Academic Achievement: Implications for Culturally Responsive Curriculum, Instruction, and Assessment. *Journal of Negro Education, 67*(3), 302-317.

Soar, R. (1977). An integration of findings from studies of teacher effectiveness. In G. Borich & K. Fenton (Eds.), *The appraisal of teaching: Concepts and process* (pp. 96-103). Reading, MA.: Addison Wesley.

Soar, R., & Soar, R. (1979). Emotional climate and management. In P. Peterson & H. Walberg (Eds.), *Research on teaching: Concepts, findings, and implications* (pp. 97-119). Berekeley, CA: McCutchan.

Spector, S. (1955). Teacher Reactions to Conflict Situations. *Journal of Educational Psychology, 46*(7), 437-445.

Sprick, R., Garrison, M., & Howard, L. (1998). *CHAMPs: A proactive and positive approach to classroom management for grades k-9.* Longmont, CO: Sopris West.

Spring, J. (2001). *Deculturalization and the Struggle for Equality: A brief history of the education of dominated cultures in the United States* (3rd). Boston: McGraw Hill.

St. John, N. (1971). Thirty-Six Teachers: Their Characteristics and Outcomes for Black and White Pupils. *American Educational Research Journal, 8(4)*, 635-648.

Stanworth, M. (1983). *Gender and Schooling: A study of sexual division in the classroom.* London: Hutchison.

Stienberg, L., Dornbusch, S., & Brown, B. (1992). Ethnic Differences in Adolescent Achievement: An Ecological Perspective. *American Psychologist, 47*(6), 723-729.

Suarez-Orozco, M. (1989). *Central American Refugees and US High Schools: A Psychological Study of*

*Motivation and Achievement.* Stanford, CA: Stanford University Press.

Sue, S., & Okazi, S. (1990). Asian-American educational achievements: A phenomenon in search of an explanation. *American Psychologist, 45(8)*, 913-920.

Sullivan, R. (1992). It's a Hit: Humor in Teaching. *Vocational Education Journal, 67*(3), 36-38.

Tapia, J. (1998). The Schooling of Puerto Ricans: Philadelphia's Most Impoverished Community. *Anthropology & Education Quarterly, 29*(3), 297-323.

TenHouton, W. (1971). Cognitive styles and social order. *Final Report, Part 2, OEO, Book - 5135.* Los Angeles: University of California.

Tennis, G., & Dabbs, J. (1975). Sex, setting, and personal space: Fist grade through college. *Sociometry, 38*, 385-394.

Timmerman, L. (1995). Rhetorical Dimensions of Teaching Effectiveness. *ED386761.*

Torrance, E. (1982). Identifying and Capitalizing on the Strengths of Culturally Different Children. In C. Reynolds & T. Gutkin (Eds.), *The Handbook of School Psychology* (pp. 481-500). New York: John Wiley & Sons.

Twenge, J., & Croker, J. (2002). Race and Self-Esteem: Meta-Analysis Comparing Whites, Blacks, Hispanics, Asians, and American Indians and Comment on Gray-Little and Hafdahl (2000). *Psychological Bulletin, 128*(3), 371-408.

US Commission on Civil Rights. (1973). Teachers and Students: Differences in Teacher Interaction with Mexican American and Anglo Students. Mexican American Education. *ED073881.*

Valverde, L. (2006). *Improving Schools for Latinos: Creating Better Learning Environments.* Lanham, MD: Rowman & Littlefield Education.

Vance, C. (1987). A Comparative Study on the Use of Humor in the Design of Instruction. *Instructional Science, 16(1)*, 79-100.

Victoria, J. (1970). An investigation of nonverbal behavior of student teachers: Final Report. *ED042742.*

Villegas, A. (1991). Culturally responsive pedagogy for the 1990s and beyond: Trends and Issues Paper No. 6. *ED339698.*

Vitto, J. (2003). *Relationship Driven Classroom Management: Strategies that promote student motivation.* Thousand Oaks, CA: Corwin Press.

Walberg, H. (1976). Psychology of learning environments: Behavioral, structure, or perceptual? In L. Shulman (Ed.), *Review of research in education* (Vol. 4, pp. 142-178). Itasca, Ill.: Peacock.

Waller, W. (1932). *Sociology of Teaching.* New York: John and Wiley and Sons.

Washington, V. (1982). Racial Differences in Teacher Perceptions of First and Fourth Grade Pupils on

Selected Characteristics. *Journal of Negro Education, 51*(1), 60-72.

Wassermann, S. (1992). Asking the Right Question: The Essence of Teacher Fastback 343. *ED355234.*

Waxman, H. (1989). Urban black and Hispanic elementary school students' perceptions of classroom instruction. *Journal of Research and Development in Education, 22(2)*, 57-61.

Weiner, L. (2003). Why is Classroom Management So Vexing to Urban Teachers? *Theory into Practice, 42*(4), 305-312.

Weinstein, R. (1983). Student Perceptions of Schooling. *Elementary School Journal, 83(4)*, 287-312.

Whitney, J., Leonard, M., Leonard, W., Camelio, M., & Camelio, V. (2005). Seek balance, connect with others, and reach all students: High school students describe a moral imperative for teachers. *High School Journal, 89*(2), 29-38.

Willis, F. (1966). Initial speaking distance as a function of the speakers' relationship. *Psychoanalytic Science, 5*, 221-222.

Willis, S., & Brophy, J. (1974). Origins of teachers' attitudes towards young children. *Journal of Educational Psychology, 66(4).*

Winne, P., & Marx, R. (1977). Re conceptualizing research on teaching. *Journal of Educational Psychology, 69(6)*, 668-678.

Wragg, C. (1995). Classroom Management: The Perspectives of Teachers, Pupils, and Researcher. *ED384578.*

Wubberhorst, J., Graford, S., & Willis, F. (1971). Trust in children as a function of race, sex, and socioeconomic group. *Psychological Reports, 29*, 1181-1187.

Young, V. (1974). A black American socialization pattern. *American Ethnologist, 1*(2), 406-413.

Zayas, L., & Solari, F. (1994). Early Childhood Socialization in Hispanic Families: Context, Culture, and Practice Implication Professional Psychology: Research Journal and Practice. *American Psychological Association, 25*(3), 200-206.

www.ingramcontent.com/pod-product-compliance
Lightning Source LLC
Chambersburg PA
CBHW060954230426
43665CB00015B/2197